Music in Film and Video Productions

Music in Film and Video Productions

Dan Carlin, Sr.

Focal Press
Boston   London

Focal Press is an imprint of Butterworth-Heinemann.

Recognizing the importance of preserving what has been written, it is the policy of Butterworth-Heinemann to have the books it publishes printed on acid-free paper, and we exert our best efforts to that end.

All pictures photographed by Christine Ogden, except Moviola on page 112 and three-quarter-inch video on page 117; both by Gene Arias.

Library of Congress Cataloging-in-Publication Data

Carlin, Dan.
  Music in film and video productions / by Dan Carlin, Sr.
    p.   cm.
  Includes index.
  ISBN 0-240-80009-5 (pbk.)
    1. Motion picture music—Instruction and study. 2. Music videos—Production and direction. 3. Sound recordings—Production and direction. 4. Music trade. I. Title.
  MT737.C3   1991
  778.5′2344—dc20   90-40741
                                                              CIP
                                                               MN

British Library Cataloguing in Publication Data

Carlin, Dan
  Music in film and video productions.
  1. Cinema films. Videorecordings. Music
  I. Title
  781.542

  ISBN 0-240-80009-5

Butterworth-Heinemann
80 Montvale Avenue
Stoneham, MA 02180

10 9 8 7 6 5 4 3 2 1

Printed in the United States of America

Dedicated to
the late Jerry Fielding

Contents

Preface

I hope that this book will serve the novitiate, as well as the professional filmmaker and video producer, as a guide to preplanning and properly preparing any and all music involved in a film or videotape project. It is an attempt to furnish enough historical and technical information to satisfy questions while also offering a complete guide to musical procedures that take us from preproduction through production and terminate with the completion of the postproduction phase.

My desire to explain these complexities started with my lecturing for the Academy of Motion Picture Arts and Sciences. The Academy, among its various philanthropic activities, sponsors a Visiting Artist Program, which includes producers, directors, writers, actors, cinematographers, sound engineers, art directors, and composers, as well as editors of film, videotape, sound effects, and music.

This program enables the Academy to send their foremost specialists to universities, colleges, and privately endowed foundations, both in the United States and abroad, to participate and lecture in symposia on film and videotape productions. As a participant in the Visiting Artist Program, I have been asked many intriguing questions regarding procedures, equipment, costs, differences between film and videotape, and other aspects of the integration of music into film and videotape programs. The need to explore and explain the various pitfalls and booby traps has been impressed upon me by questioning audiences and by producers, directors, and composers actively working in the industry. The procedures for acquiring music, the many options available when using music on the set, the addition of underscore to a project, and the expense involved will be explored. The aim is to do it correctly in order to save time and money and, more important, to ensure that creative options will not be impaired by the mismanagement of the many details involved when integrating music.

This is a pragmatic study of the materials and the procedures to follow in order to facilitate options when dealing with recorded music or music that is about to be recorded. We will not attempt an analysis or critique of any composers or specific music. Analyzing the subtleties of original underscore music for the emotional enhancement of a motion picture means studying the sensitivity and artistry of the great composers who are responsible for the development of this art form. Their creative genius stands apart in an ivory tower of sorts. As filmmakers or videotape producers and directors, you do not have to move into that tower; you only have to know that the musical scores floating down from its parapets must be dealt with in terms of musicians, scoring stages, contractors, copyists, librarians, music editors, scoring mixers, music clearance houses, and the like.

This is our topic—the mundane avenues that one must travel to and from the ivory tower of creativity to ensure that the proper procedures are followed in planning and executing the integration of source and underscore music into a film or videotape production.

Acknowledgments

Thanks to:

My spouse, Elizabeth, for her help, critical analysis, moral support, and patience.

Four offspring—Daniel, Thomas, Kathryn, and Patricia. For their encouragement, and for just being, I am indeed grateful.

Randy Honaker, for brochures that explained in greater detail those elements I would have treated in a cavalier manner.

Don Wilkins, for his helpful suggestions and critique.

Phil Sutherland, who organized and edited this work.

And Jerry Fielding. All of us who knew, worked with, and loved Jerry carry a standard that bears the question: "What would Jerry think about this?" That question is posed at executive board meetings of the Music Branch of the Academy of Motion Picture Arts and Sciences, at spotting sessions, on scoring stages, in casual conversations between friends regarding social issues, and as a criterion of other composers' work.

This book is the direct result of Jerry Fielding coercing a music editor out of a cutting room and pushing him into the lecture halls and classrooms of brilliant young cinema art students across the country.

It's a little better world because of Jerry Fielding.

· 1 ·

Music and the Stages of a Production

THE PRIMARY TYPES OF FILM AND VIDEO MUSIC

There are two main types of music in productions, each distinguished by its relationship to the action in the film or video. *Source music* emanates from a visual source within the film narrative—for example, an actor singing, whistling, or humming on camera; a musical group with a visual or nonvisual performance; a radio, jukebox, music box, calliope, organ grinder, or Muzak. The other category of music is *underscore music*, which is written and recorded specifically for individual scenes after the completion of the picture. Underscore music has no definable source within the picture and is designed to enhance the emotion of the picture in a less conspicuous way.

Both types of music can and should be a fundamental component of a successful film or video. To that end, music must be carefully planned and properly integrated into the production. Because of its origin within the film narrative, source music usually is created as part of the shooting script or production stage of a film or video. Underscore is usually created and integrated later, after the visual (picture) component of the film or video has been edited.

All film and videotape productions are divided into three phases: preproduction, production or shooting, and postproduction.

PREPRODUCTION

Preproduction encompasses many activities. The script, after polishing by the writer, producer, and director, is broken down into a daily shooting schedule according to scenes, script pages, location sites, and the actors' availability and contractual commitments. This schedule should reflect some shooting flexibility for the indoor or exterior scenes to allow for inclement weather. The casting and contracting of actors must take place. A cinematographer, art director, film or videotape editor, production manager, and compatible staff are assembled. Scouting for locations, obtaining shooting permits, building and decorating sets, acquiring wardrobe, preparing special effects—these are all prerequisites to implementing the structure and requirements of the script. If, in the preproduction meetings, planning and instrumentation are meticulous, then logistics will be smooth and fewer obstacles will exist for the producer, director, cast, and crew on the production set.

For most pictures, a limited amount of music work is required at this stage. The producer and director need to visualize, if only generally, the final film or video so that they can effectively plan for music and anticipate its budget and other requirements. At some point they will need to hire a composer, music coordinator, music editor, and other music staff whose abilities are consistent with their goals.

However, productions with source music may require much more planning, particularly if the production includes a musical performance. Personnel normally involved later, in postproduction, such as the composer and music editor, would then begin their work during preproduction.

Occasionally, when the script calls for a musical improvisation, this seems so simple that it is easily glossed over in preproduction planning. But the arrival of that music in the postproduction phase may assault producers and directors in the most unlikely manner. There is no other area so loaded with complexities and hidden expense as a simple piece of music.

PRODUCTION

The second phase, referred to as *production*, begins as the camera starts rolling and the assistant director on the first day's shoot calls, "Roll 'em." (It's the director who yells, "Action!") The director, as the creative decision maker in charge, is ultimately responsible for every frame of film photographed. This is not to say that the formidable crew of experts who dress and light the stage, the camera crew who photograph the action, and the sound recordist's crew are exempt from responsibility, but a smoothly running production and a happy cast and crew are a reflection of the director's ability to organize and bring forth everyone's best efforts.

After the first day's shooting is completed, the exposed negative is sent to a film laboratory for development, and the preferred takes are printed. For film, the set recordist's tapes are sent to the sound transfer department, where they are transferred to 35 mm single-stripe; in the case of videotape, the preferred takes are transferred to a one-inch master tape. Either way, the production shooting of the previous day is viewed by the producer, director, director of photography, editor, assistant editor, and anyone else invited by the producer to attend. At this viewing there is a constant analysis of the material from a dramatic and technical viewpoint. Decisions are made to reshoot scenes for camera angles or framing, lighting defects, out-of-focus shots, or dramatic content.

The production phase continues through the day-by-day shooting of the script in the studio or on location. It ends on the last day of shooting, when the director yells: "Cut and print—that's a wrap!"

POSTPRODUCTION

Postproduction, the final phase, represents the fruition of all of the previous efforts. The film or videotape editor, who has been assembling sequences as they were shot (not necessarily in the order of the script), now assembles the entire picture in script continuity. This initial assembly is called a *first cut*. The producer and director, together with the editor, will meticulously analyze the first cut. Usually the production will be over length, necessitating that scenes be shortened or dropped completely. Other scenes might be transposed, stock footage may be added, and editing continues until the picture flows with timing and grace.

When the polishing is complete and the production is within the proper playing time, the picture assistant will order the opticals (any special effects requiring specialized processing) and integrate them into the production. The picture is now considered in *final cut*. At this point the main and end titles can be designed and ordered. A composer and music editor are called in for a *music spotting session* with the director, producer, and picture editor, during which they will collectively select those scenes to be enhanced with underscore music.

A sound effects and a dialogue editor will view the picture with the director, producer, and picture editor to discuss the sound effects, original dialogue lines to be rerecorded, and any additional wild lines (nonvisual or off-stage lines) needed.

During the period from the completion of the final cut to the day when the rerecording or sweetening (blending all sound components) begins, music is written and recorded; the usable production dialogue tracks are cleaned of extraneous noises; sound effects and music units are built; and, in film, the original negative is cut. The rerecorded dialogue sections that replace the existing hard-to-hear lines and any changes in readings, along with the duplicated stage movements of the actors with ambient background tracks to fill under the new material, are built into units, readying the picture for the rerecording stage.

On the rerecording or sweetening stage, the dialogue, sound effects, and music units (reels of film or tape containing a type of sound element) are balanced to the producer's satisfaction while being rerecorded on their own individual *stems* (tracks or segments) of magnetic tape. These three elements are again transferred to make either an optical composite track, a stereo track, or a multi-surround track negative. This optical sound track negative is sent to the film laboratory for development and, by putting it together with the cut negative, a first-trial answer print is made. In the case of a videotape, no optical negative is necessary. A composite of the sweetened sound track is transferred to the one-inch edited video master.

The first-trial answer print or video master is viewed by the director and producer to ensure that the color is corrected and absolutely perfect before any additional prints or videotapes are made for theatrical or television release.

This completes a cursory outline of the three phases of the making of a film or videotape program.

· 2 ·

Credit Titles

KNOWING WHO EVERYBODY IS

An incredible number of people are involved in the production of a motion picture. Each individual has a special niche to fill, which includes a title, a specific range of duties and often an impact on the production's musical decisions. Although not everyone has the same degree of influence, it is important to know what the major positions are.

EXECUTIVE PRODUCER

Usually the first title credit to be seen on a film or videotape production is executive producer—a formidable title for the one individual who holds overall responsibility for the total production. The executive producer might have sold the original concept for the film or television series to the studio or network with the stipulation that he or she will be retained as executive producer. A staff member of a studio can be designated as the executive producer by the studio head.

The responsibilities of the executive producer are the same for television and for feature films. All the principal actors, director, line producer, director of photography, set designers, set decorators, production manager, assistant director, editors, composer, and every other important position must be approved by the executive producer.

He will view and critique the *dailies* (West Coast term) or *rushes* (East Coast term), the previous day's shooting, not only to critique the actors' performances but also to examine technical aspects such as direction, number of camera setups, camera angles, coverage of scenes, lighting, set decoration, and anything else that might influence the final production.

The responsibility to establish and then remain within a budget is the executive producer's. Business contracts and dealings with agents, publicity departments, film exhibitors, art title design, special screenings, previews, promotion—everything and anything questionable is delivered to the executive producer for a decision. The executive producer has the final word on the dubbing or sweetening stage regarding the dialogue, music, and effects.

LINE PRODUCER

A *line producer* has more hands-on responsibilities in dealing with the shooting set. She represents the authority on the set for emergency consultation regarding anything that goes awry or needs an executive decision in an improvisational situation. If a director feels the picture needs a scenic exploitation shot, but only a helicopter can accomplish this feat, the line producer must make an immediate decision based on any number of given factors: Will the shot add to the aesthetic value of the film? Will it delay the production schedule? Is it worth the rental cost to keep the director happy? How much trouble will she be in with the executive producer if she says yes? Worse yet, how much trouble will she be in if she says no?

The line producer handles important monetary decisions as she constantly observes the progress of the filming in relation to the preplanned schedule. She steps in to push things along if it appears they are falling behind schedule. The line producer will be the one who ensures that a playback operator and proper equipment are scheduled for the day when music is needed on the set. The line producer also keeps the executive producer apprised of progress and morale on the set.

DIRECTOR

The *director* is the visual interpreter of the script, the one who brings the story to life on the screen. The lifeblood of the script can be as sterile or as fertile as the imagination and creativity of the director. Those directors who achieve greatness do so because of their sensitivity to emotional situations and their ability to incorporate the subtle nuances of ordinary day-to-day living activities. That background extra who wanders up, eating an apple, to watch an argument between the principals on a street corner gives the scene a touch of humanity that it otherwise would lack.

More and more, directors are wearing two hats—that of the producer as well as the director's. This gives them much more creative control and eliminates the possible influence or interference of another party. Directors' contracts are changing, also, and may include such items as a director's cut, a preselected composer, one or two previews, a screen credit reading "A [Director's Name] Picture," and the like. This type of contract gives directors their selection of all the principal individuals involved, supervision of the editing, their choice of a dubbing stage, supervision of the final dub, and selection of the area and theater to preview the picture. The director is almost 100 percent responsible for either the smooth functioning of musical sequences or the inept handling of the music on the shooting set.

ASSOCIATE PRODUCER

The specific role of an *associate producer* is nebulous, as there is no specific delineation of the services involved. The title indicates that this individual aids the producer. This aid can take the form of keeping a fresh supply of coffee available at all times. But this individual could also really be performing some of the important functions of a producer who is spread too thin with other projects. The norm falls somewhere between these extremes. A diversity of demands—from preproduction planning, to the activities on the shooting set, through the final dub, and then through expediting the film through the laboratories—usually keeps an associate producer running constantly. The associate producer can be involved with the music research and clearances when music is used in the production shooting.

COMPOSER

A *composer* is a person who writes music. A *film composer* is a person who specializes in writing music for the visual medium, whether it be film or video productions. This art form is highly specialized. The technique of writing music that will be compatible with dialogue and effects and still underscore (instill in the audience) the emotions of a scene is not to be taken lightly. There are two distinct forms of film music. One form includes the current recordings of popular music performers in the entertainment business. The other form of music is specifically written for the emotional enhancement of a pictorial scene. Film composers walk a fine line by creating up-to-date sounds yet subjugating their music to the dramatic content of a production. A mistake often made by filmmakers in an effort to be original and do something daring is to contract a popular music group or an outstanding commercial recording artist to compose underscore music for their project. This is like asking a dermatologist to perform an appendectomy. The desire on the part of some studio executives and independent producers to have a potentially commercially successful song or songs written for their picture is understandable. But it's better to limit the talents of the commercial performing group to the main or end title and allow those with the expertise to write the underscore.

CHOREOGRAPHER

The *choreographer,* a seldom-seen credit unless the production includes a dance routine, is responsible for creating a dance routine that will be unique for the film or video. She will confer with the director to establish the emotional and dramatic intent of the routine, and will give input to both the set designer and the set decorator concerning needed area and props. She will supervise and instruct the dancers in the routine she develops and work with the composer regarding tempo, arrangement of the music, and its embellishments.

SCRIPT SUPERVISOR

The *script supervisor* is the meticulous observer and log keeper on the set. Every time the camera rolls, the script supervisor starts a stopwatch to record the overall time of the scene. He lists it as a master shot, two-shot, close-up, over-shoulder, and so on, and indicates on the script by lines what slate and take number is covering what areas. The script supervisor also watches to ensure that if three people exit a doorway in a particular order, they enter the next room in the same order when the camera is repositioned for their entrance. It is an extraordinarily responsible position. Observant as the script supervisor can be, there will be some mis-matches when cutting from master shots to other angles. A glass that was being held in the hand on one shot will be on the table for the pickup, a hat being worn by a principal will now be on the left instead of the right side, cigarettes will change in length and position. No one can catch everything, but the script supervisor tries. It is this individual who will have logged the slates that have music playbacks and will have indicated the print takes.

PICTURE EDITOR

The *picture editor* assembles the dailies as the shooting progresses. The previous day's shooting, after being viewed by those members of the crew who have been invited or instructed to attend the screening of dailies, will be logged and coded by the assistant editor and then presented to the editor for an assembly. This assembly is not necessarily in order of the shooting script. The editor assembles the scenes as shot and, when the production phase is complete, will edit the material together in the proper sequence as dictated by the script. This is considered the first cut and is usually over length. (It had better be or the director is in trouble!) From this point on, the editor works with the director and producer to create the final product. When musical sequences are involved, the picture editor will deliver the scenes with music to the music editor for special coding in order to intercut scenes in playback sync.

POSTPRODUCTION SUPERVISOR

The *postproduction supervisor* oversees the scheduling of the entire postproduction operation. This includes making an educated guess about the date of the final cut and then creating a schedule to encompass all the activities necessary to the completion of the film. The postproduction supervisor has the task of bargaining and making arrangements with the management of laboratories and art title houses. He or she is the immediate supervisor of the music editor, and is also responsible for sound effects editorial, the dubbing stage, the scoring stage, the Automated Dialogue Replacement (ADR) and Foley stages, the negative cutting facilities, and the release prints. Finally, working up a budget for the entire cost of this postproduction operation also falls on the shoulders of this individual.

MUSIC SUPERVISOR

The *music supervisor* can best be defined as the person who has knowledge of and some connections with the recording industry. The music supervisor studies the script with the producer and director to get their feelings about the type of music they want— whether to use classical or pop tunes, and whether those tunes should be rendered as instrumentals or vocals to best evoke the time period of the production. The list might include a recording by the Ink Spots for a feeling of the 1940s, of Elvis Presley for the 1950s, or of the Beatles for the 1960s. After a decision is made, the music supervisor contacts the publisher and the recording companies of the selected tunes to establish a price for a sync license granting the production company the right to use a piece of music in a film or video production. The license can be multifaceted and complex, permitting use of the music only in certain ways and under certain conditions. Licensing is obviously a very important part of incorporating music into a film or video production. The price for the license can vary tremendously on the basis of the way the chosen tune will be used in the production, the popularity of the tune in today's market, the recording company's contractual commitment to the artist who performed the tune, and the market in which the production will be exhibited. In this instance, the principal function of the music supervisor is the selection and negotiation of price for the songs to be used in the production.

The music supervisor can also be responsible for selecting musicians or a musical group who will prerecord for a playback or give a live performance on the shooting set. The music supervisor's input regarding musicians and musical groups, as well as his or her knowledge of the correct recording and set procedures, makes this person invaluable on the production set.

The title of music supervisor gives the impression that this individual oversees all the music, but this is not true. The music supervisor has nothing to do with the supervision of a composer. Nonetheless, it is a title that is easily misinterpreted and infringes on the status prestige of a composer. Music supervisors for film production companies have overcome the disdain from composers by changing their credit to read *music consultant* or *music coordinator*. A person with any of the three credits may also function as a *music contractor*.

MUSIC COORDINATOR

A *music coordinator*, under the auspices of a composer, will make a budget based on the number of minutes of music to be recorded and the type of orchestra required to meet the needs of the picture. The budget is based on the ideal situation with everything running smoothly, but with contingency planning for the expectation that anything that can possibly go wrong, will. If the music coordinator is familiar with the rate of the recording time normally used by a composer, and knows that the producer and director have not made too many requests for changes in music on the scoring stage in the past, then the estimated budget can come reasonably close to the actual costs.

MUSIC CONTRACTOR

A music contractor estimates a budget for the entire music package, makes reservations for a scoring stage, calls the musicians for the scoring dates, and is present on the score to ensure the correct reporting of the musicians' playing time and their instrumental doubling. Acting as the orchestra manager, he or she also calls the rest breaks and ensures that union regulations are followed. The responsibility for instrument rental and cartage falls on the music contractor's shoulders.

MUSIC EDITOR

The music editor works with a composer through the scoring of the picture, and then acts as the composer's representative on dubbing stage, supervising and protecting the integrity of the score.

The music editor is present with the composer at the spotting session, where starts and stops of the music to cover underscored scenes are selected. These spotting notes are the basis of the breakdown notes, which are extremely detailed, describing in terms of seconds and tenths of seconds the action and dialogue in every scene to be underscored. As the composer completes a cue and sends meter, tempo, and streamer information to the music editor, that cue is prepared on film or videotape for the scoring stage. On the scoring stage, the editor slates the individual pieces of music by scene and take number, operates the digital metronome that sends the clicks to the orchestra, activates the seconds clock, makes note of the type of music that has been recorded (love, tension, chase, fight, time passing, and so on), and times each recording. The recorded material is then prepared by the music editor for the rerecording or sweetening stage. The editor remains on the rerecording or sweetening stage to make any sophistications or changes requested by the director or producer.

The last operation for the music editor is the completion of a music report, listing all the music used in the final rerecording, which is then sent to the production office.

PRODUCTION MIXER

The production mixer is responsible for the quality of the sound recorded on the shooting set. He or she keeps a log of all recorded scenes, which also include any music playbacks.

MUSIC ENGINEER

The music engineer balances the entire orchestra on the scoring session and assigns instruments and instrumental sections to specific tracks on the multitape.

MUSIC RECORDIST

The music recordist operates the multitrack recording machine and notes all track assignments on a log.

· 3 ·

Fundamentals of Film Sound and Music

THE ORIGINS OF FILM MUSIC

Early in this century, filmmakers realized that the films being shown in Nickelodeon theaters would be a lot more effective with a musical accompaniment. Filmmakers hired composers to write piano compositions for these short epics. The music was composed, printed out, and distributed along with the film. The theater owner would hire a local pianist to read the sheet music and play the piano while watching the film for visual cues. As films gained in popularity and length, some theater owners embellished this procedure with an organ accompaniment. Eventually, there were complete orchestral arrangements played by pit orchestras to underscore the silent movies.

Next, filmmakers began distributing big phonograph recordings of full orchestras with their films. These "platters" were given to a projectionist, who would operate the phonograph player, dropping the needle at predetermined sync points.

Then came the "talkies"—movies with a sound track. A way had been found to photograph sound waves. As a scene was being shot on a set, another piece of unexposed film was running along at

17

the same speed as the camera, photographing the sound waves of the dialogue and ambient sounds on the set. (The first type was a variable-density sound track; the second type, still used today on optical release prints, is the variable-area sound track.) Because the camera and sound recording equipment were interlocked, they were in perfect synchronization, or sync. With this recording system, once the film was in final cut (when the editing phase was completely finished), sound effect tracks and music tracks could also be placed in sync with the picture on a stage where the individual volume of the sounds could be controlled, adjusted, blended, and then rerecorded (photographed onto a new sound track).

Then magnetic tape recorders came on the scene. The ability to record on magnetic tape involved much less expense and easier-to-handle equipment, while recording cleaner, sharper sound. This development inspired the sound engineers to research and develop a tape recorder that could be used on a shooting set.

This is now the means by which sound is recorded for most film or video productions. Although new developments, including digital recording, are now appearing on the horizon, most of the fundamental methods and processes remain the same.

MAGNETIC RECORDING TAPE

Standard film has an area for recorded sound. On a film shooting set, however, sound cannot be recorded on the picture film as is done with videotape. The film production set mixer is recording dialogue on magnetic tape. After this dialogue tape is transferred to magnetic film, the assistant editor puts it in sync with the picture for viewing and editing purposes. Along with effects and music tracks, this same track, after postproduction dubbing or sweetening is completed, is combined on the dubbing stage to magnetic film, transferred to optical, and then imprinted on the sound track area of the picture that is released to the theaters. Up to this point, all sound is recorded and processed on magnetic tape.

Magnetic recording tape is fundamentally similar to videotape. A magnetically sensitive emulsion, often composed of an oxide compound, is applied to a plastic ribbon. Videotape has two standard recording tracks, allowing for a stereo version or for dialogue on one track and the music and effects on another, and a third channel, termed an address track, that may be used for SMPTE time code.

Recording tapes, quarter-inch, half-inch, one-inch, and two-inch, have as many variables as there are recording machines. A quarter-inch tape may be used to record a single track or stereo. A half-inch tape, the standard in the industry for four-track analog sound, now has the capacity for 48-track digital recording, while a one-inch tape, developed for an eight-track analog recorder, is used by a 32-track digital recorder. The two-inch track, developed for the obsolescent 16-track recorder, is now used for 24-track, either of which is analog sound.

Recording to two channels is termed *stereo recording*. Recording to more than two channels is termed *multitrack recording*. As previously noted, magnetic recording tape is also in the format of 35 mm film-based sprocketed stock, which can accommodate from one to six channels of sound. This allows it to be easily synchronized with film.

Because sound and music are recorded separately from the visual part of a film or video, it is vital that there be some means by which those sound elements can be synchronized with the picture. This has been a problem in the past and still can be one at times, but there are solutions.

SYNCHRONOUS PULSE

If you play a record on your turntable while timing it with a stopwatch, and then play it and time it again on another turntable, there will be a slight variance in the overall timing. Even if the difference is only a few seconds, one second represents 24 frames in 35 mm film, and 30 frames in videotape. This deviation is totally unacceptable when synchronizing the sound and picture is a necessity.

Suppose a quarter-inch tape is used to record sound on the set, and the sound department then has to transfer that tape to a single-stripe magnetic 35 mm film so that the picture editor will have sound with the picture. Without some sort of speed control, that transfer operation would have the same effect as playing your record a second time on a different machine: It will not be exactly the same length. This was the challenge that had to be resolved: how to maintain the identical speed of the quarter-inch set recording tape when it is placed on a transfer machine to make a single-stripe 35 mm magnetic film to be used in sync with the picture.

Early on, before sound, a similar problem was applicable to the film speed of the camera. If the shutter speed of a camera on a shooting set is not consistent at 24 frames per second, the true speed of the original photography will not be duplicated when the film is projected. When a director calls for a slow-motion shot, the camera is adjusted to run at double speed or whatever increased increment is requested. The motion becomes slow only when the film is projected at the standard 24 frames per second.

The stabilization of the camera's speed with a projection machine was the first challenge. That was remedied with a quartz crystal oscillator. The quartz crystal oscillates or filters a constant electrical frequency output, thereby ensuring a smooth and consistent flow of power to the camera motor regardless of the power source (wall plug, batteries, or generator). Thus, the engineers stabilized the operating speed of a camera to register a consistent movement of 24 frames per second. The 35 mm negative in a camera has sprocket holes to maintain proper framing and to control slippage. Not so with the quarter-inch recording tape. A quarter-inch tape machine is mechanically driven by capstans, roller-based transport mechanisms, and therefore is not as exacting or as controllable. Even if the electric motors were running at a constant speed, it does not allow for slippage or tape stretching. Given the nature of the capstan drive, and the lack of sprocket holes in the quarter-inch tape, there is no way that engineers could mechanically synchronize the sound track with the camera. Other avenues had to be explored. With the mechanics eliminated as a source of solving the challenge, the only other element involved was the quarter-inch tape itself.

Again the quartz crystal oscillator saved the day. Installing a quartz crystal oscillator in the quarter-inch tape recorder not only stabilized the speed; at the same time, it recorded a constant 60-cycle pulsation on an isolated area of the tape that would not interfere with the sound recording.

With this pulse on the production mixer's quarter-inch track, when the tape is delivered on the sound transfer facility, the running speed of the sound transfer machine is now governed by the sync pulse. The transfer machine exactly duplicates the original speed by maintaining a consistent reading of 60 cycles from the recorded sync pulse on the quarter-inch tape. Any transfer machine with a quartz crystal reader will produce a print with the exact timing of the original quarter-inch production tape by monitoring the sync pulse to control the speed. Without a sync pulse, there would always be a variable speed factor.

The sync pulse in recording tape performs a function similar to that of the control track in videotape.

Any time you think it would probably be all right to slip a piece of music into your production without having a referenced master print with a sync pulse, SMPTE time code (SMPTE stands for the Society of Motion Picture and Television Engineers), or sprocket magnetic film as a master, rest assured that you will have to pay for your decision in time, money, and artistic compromise.

ANALOG VERSUS DIGITAL RECORDING

There are currently two main methods by which sound is recorded on tape. The older, and still more prevalent, of the two is analog recording. Sound consists of series of waves of air molecules; the nature of the sound depends strongly on the fluctuating strength, or amplitude, of the sound. Sound is inherently analog in nature. In analog recording, the tape electronically retains the fluctuating amplitude of the sound. The sound reproduced from the recording is a facsimile of the original sound. As with any copy, however, each generation of reproduction suffers some degree of degradation, even with the best recording equipment. This is a particular problem for film and video productions, where high quality is an absolute necessity and many generations of recording may be needed before a final sound track can be achieved.

The development of digital technology produced a much more accurate method of recording and reproducing sound. Digital recording equipment receives an analog sound signal and converts it to a series of values or numbers. The equipment divides the range of possible sound amplitudes into sections, with each section possessing a value. The system also divides the duration of the sound into tiny intervals of time, measuring (sampling) the sound's strength within each interval. The smaller the intervals and the more numerous the sections in which the amplitude is divided, the more precise the recording. Top-quality equipment is extremely precise.

In digital recording, then, precise values, rather than a facsimile of the original sound, are recorded. Not only can digital recording be of superior quality, but because only numbers are being copied, there is no degradation between generations. There are still unresolved concerns in using digital technology, but it is very likely that digital technology will increasingly become the industry standard.

FILM TO VIDEO TRANSFER

Film to video transfer is an increasingly important part of modern production. Even if film is the medium in which a production is ultimately released to theaters, because it is so easy to play and reference videotape, copies are used in many phases of postproduction. In addition, film is transferred to videotape for home video release and television broadcast.

Special devices called telecine machines are used for this conversion process. There are two different high-quality telecine machines that are used to transfer film to videotape. One is a Rank Cintel that transfers film to video at 23.98 frames per second to duplicate the running time of the NTSC (National Television System Committee) standard. The other, called a Film Chain, operates at the standard projection speed of 24 frames per second.

A telecine operation involves transferring film to video in either a drop or a nondrop format. The telecine machine can originate and burn in a visible SMPTE time code on the video frames (sometimes called a window dub) while placing the film sound track and the invisible SMPTE into preselected audio channels. Burning in a 35 mm feet and frame count is also an option. When transferring film to videotape, in order to be certain the videotape duplicates the running time of the film, the film being transferred to video may be slowed from a 60-cycle reference to the running speed of the video; 59.94. With this slowed-down film transfer, the timings on the film and the videotape will match each other, cut for cut and frame for frame. However, this is not the true running time of the film. When the film is projected on the dubbing stage at its normal speed, any music that has been scored to video, when run at standard film speed, will be over length. If you have scored to videotape, the music, after it has been recorded, must be speeded up to 60 cycles during the transfer operation in order to match the running time of the projected film on the dubbing stage. If the underscore music has been recorded to video and is to be rerecorded on a video sweetening stage, the music will fit perfectly without any adjustment. The process of increasing the speed of the transfer machine from 59.94- to 60-cycle Hertz has so little effect on the sound or pitch of the music as to be undetectable.

For a music editor to ensure that the timings taken from a videotape are correct, information from the video transfer house must be obtained to ascertain the format, either drop or nondrop time code. The speed of the telecine machine, 23.98 or 24 frames per second, is also a factor for the timing notes. The computer that is used to convert the video timings to true time for the composer's breakdown notes must be preprogrammed for both the film transfer speed and drop or nondrop format.

Britain and some members of the Commonwealth, along with Europe, use a 50-cycle sync pulse. Their film and their videotape are projected at 25 frames per second. This videotape format is referred to as phase alternating line, commonly referred to as the PAL system. Adjustments must be made to compensate between the different formats when programs are to be taken abroad or foreign programs brought to the United States.

In the United States, our 60-cycle system is initialized NTSC, which, as noted before, stands for the National Television System Committee.

Here is an example of the complexities that can arise from the different formats. A "Movie of the Week" was photographed in New Zealand. Because local cameras and sound equipment were used, the film was shot at 25 frames per second and the sound recordist used a 50-cycle Hertz for sync. The music sequence was made to a playback; that is, a song was recorded on the set before the photography took place. When the time came to shoot the musical number, the recording was played back and the local singers played along with the playback. This enabled the music editor to have a clean recording of the music without any dialogue or camera noise. When the film was delivered to the United States, the picture was adjusted to our standard of 24 frames per second. All of the postproduction, including the sweetening, was to take place on videotape, so the adjusted film had to be transferred to videotape.

The music editor was presented with a quarter-inch playback tape, recorded on the set at 25 frames per second with a 50-cycle sync. This quarter-inch playback had to be transferred to 35 mm magnetic film using a corrected speed ratio to match the videotape that was going to be used on the sweetening stage. The challenge presented to the editor was how to figure the speed ratio from the 25 frames at 50 Hertz to the 24 frames at 60 Hertz, while also adjusting for the slowdown from 60 to 59.94 Hertz when the film was transferred to video. Everyone who tried to figure out a formula for this one came up with a different answer.

When working on a project in which it is necessary to have the film transferred to videotape, there are several options available but only two absolute necessities: a visual SMPTE time display on the video picture, and a SMPTE time code signal on one of the other two available audio tracks.

Music editors use the SMPTE time display to get timings for a composer and to prepare the video for the scoring stage. These timings must be adjusted to either a drop or nondrop frame format, 59.94 or 60-cycle film transfer. The composer writes to the true time of the material to be scored, so all SMPTE time codes must be adjusted to reflect true time. All these necessary calculations are computerized.

Videotape is so easy to handle and so flexible in its ability to accommodate different-colored streamers (lines that go across the picture), punch marks (circles void of picture), variable click tracks (metronomic beats that increase and decrease as needed), and a myriad of other highly technical functions that even diehard music editors have been won over to this flexible and efficient format.

TOOLS AND TRACK

Technically, a production begins with the recording medium; that's what makes everything else possible. Film, though often more expensive and difficult to use, still offers a higher quality picture than videotape, and thus should remain for the foreseeable future the medium of motion pictures and many television programs. Picture film consists of a thin plastic ribbon coated with an emulsion that, when exposed to light, retains the image illuminated by the light. One side of the ribbon contains the emulsion;

this side is dull. The other, shiny side has no emulsion and is often called the *cell side*.

A production is generally shot on film negative; it is then processed so the film can retain the recorded image indefinitely. To view the recorded images, a positive print must be made. Motion pictures are created by recording on film a sequence of still images called *frames*, which, when run at a sufficient, constant speed, create the illusion of smooth motion. In standard 35 millimeter (35 mm) film, there are 16 frames per foot of film. The standard industry film speed, which efficiently produces a high-quality image, is 24 frames per second. This rate is important, as it is the basis for sound and music recording speeds for 35 mm film.

Film has small, evenly spaced perforations called *sprockets* running the length of each of its edges. These sprockets enable mechanisms in both cameras and projectors to advance the film at a regular speed. The most commonly used type of 35 mm film has four perforations on each side of each frame. When recording images, a film camera advances the film one frame at a time, exposing that frame for an instant by means of a rapidly opening and closing shutter.

Numbers run along one edge of film as a reference for developers and technicians. Other numbers may be applied to the edge as a reference for editors and other postproduction personnel. These numbers enable editors to specify cuts and assemble the film accurately.

In a standard film print shown in movie theaters, a narrow strip running along one edge of the film contains all of the sound elements. This combined picture and sound track is called a composite print, and is made at the very end of the production process. Throughout most of the production, the sound elements are separated from the picture.

Early filmmakers recorded sound optically (photographically). However, modern sound recording for both film and video uses *magnetic track* consisting of an oxidized emulsion applied to a film surface. The emulsion retains electronic signals (sound) in the form of patterns in its oxidized surface.

There are many forms of film used to record sound in this way, but three of the most important are single-stripe, three-stripe, and full-coat magnetic track. The first two offer, respectively, one and three narrow bands, also called channels or stems, of emulsion running the length of the film. Full-coat track has emulsion covering the entire width of the film. Each has its own special purposes in production.

VIDEOTAPE

Like film, videotape consists of a thin ribbon of plastic (actually polyester) coated with an emulsion. The emulsion on videotape, unlike the light-sensitive emulsion on film, is magnetically sensitive and usually composed of oxide compounds. Video images are recorded as electronic patterns in the emulsion. These patterns can then be "read" by video playback units, which recreate the original images.

There are many different types of videotape, varying in width (from 8 mm to two inches or more), method of recording and playback, image quality, and other characteristics. At the moment, one-inch videotape is the standard for creating broadcast-quality images. Smaller format tapes, such as three-quarter-inch, half-inch, and 8 mm, are improving in quality but at this point are still generally used in a production for producing "reference" tapes for key personnel.

Unlike the case of film, nothing recorded on videotape is visible to the naked eye. However, videotape is also structured in frames of electronic information, and as with film these frames are viewed sequentially at a rate fast enough to create the illusion of continuous motion. Each frame of video information is further divided into two halves, called *fields*.

Just as frames of film are identified by edge numbers, so video frames are identified by a time-based code that is part of the magnetic recording. The standard time code for video was established by the Society of Motion Picture and Television Engineers, or SMPTE (colloquially pronounced "sempty"), in 1969. This code was accepted both in the United States and Europe and has become the world standard.

SMPTE time code consists of an eight-digit number corresponding to a 60-minute clock. Four sets of two digits represent reading from left to right, hours, minutes, seconds, and frames. For example, code for a video frame might be 05:43:16:09. This format accommodates the standard recording and playback rate for video.

Videotape in its developmental stage, in a black-and-white format, ran at 30 frames per second on 60-cycle Hertz. When color video came to the forefront, the 60-cycle Hertz somehow interfered with the color bars and consequently had to be adjusted ever so slightly. This was accomplished by reducing the 60 cycles to 59.94. This adjustment created a discrepancy between true time and the SMPTE time code. The true time of 1:00 would read 00:00:59:28. In other words, the adjustment resulted in a discrepancy of two frames per minute, or approximately four seconds in an hour. The video industry compensated for this discrepancy by dropping two frame numbers of the video display as it changed over to the next minute by going from 00:00:59:29 to 00:01:00:02. This is termed *drop frame* video. You actually don't drop any visual frames, you simply skip numbers from the 29th frame of the 59th second to the 02 count of the next second. In this drop frame format, you cannot be certain of true time except when the SMPTE time code is reading the start of every minute. It slowly drifts from that exactitude as it progresses until the next minute is reached, when it drops the two frame numbers again and you're back to true time.

Experts are aware that there are other idosyncrasies in drop frame video—for example, that two frames in each minute are *not* dropped at each multiple of ten minutes. In almost all normal productions, however, the slight inaccuracies in drop frame make no difference.

The opposite of drop frame is nondrop frame video. As the name attests, the frames are not dropped, and the video is not quite time-accurate.

Most programs are videotaped completely in drop frame, so that true time (or a figure only minutely different from it), which is most important to networks, will always be displayed on their editing material. If nondrop frame is used, the SMPTE code will fall approximately one second behind every 15 minutes, and that amounts to about four seconds in a one-hour program. Add that loss over a broadcast day when commercial time is sold by the second, and it makes a big difference. Of course, nondrop can be easily adjusted to true time but, given the stakes, network executives do not want to rely on any individual's mathematical calculation of the exact running time of a program or segment thereof.

When film is going to be transferred to video in the postproduction phase for easy reference, there is no need for anything but a nondrop frame format, as the overall time is not a critical factor. Composers, sound effects editors, and music editors will order nondrop time code for their work. In any event, the video runs at the identical speed regardless of whether the SMPTE code is drop or nondrop frame.

ANATOMY OF VIDEOTAPE

Although the makeup varies somewhat by format, most professional-quality videotape contains two or three audio tracks, a control track channel, a wide channel for the video (picture) information, and perhaps auxiliary tracks. Time code carried on one of the audio tracks or on a special *address track* is called *longitudinal time code*. Time code also may be recorded as part of the video information, hidden in the unseen portion of the video frame (like the frame line in film). This is called *vertical interval time code* (VITC).

Time code numbers can remain unseen or, with special recorders, can be displayed visually in an elongated window placed at some spot in the picture. Video displaying time code in this manner is called a *window dub*. Videotape editors use this displayed time code to reference picture edits and program them on computers.

The control track is a very important part of the videotape. It consists of evenly spaced electronic pulses by which a recorder can monitor the tape's recording or playback speed and maintain it. Control track permits the maintenance of consistent speed for video as sprocket holes do for film.

Sound effects editors will transfer the code itself for reference purposes to recording tape and then prepare dialogue, backgrounds, and effects for either the sweetening or the dubbing stage.

Music editors reference the SMPTE time code for the spotting notes and breakdown timing notes to be sent to a composer in preparation for scoring. The videotape usually will be used for the scoring of a film or video program.

Composers use the video as a constant frame of reference while writing the score. It is invaluable for refreshing their memory of the mood of a scene and also for playing against the video to see if the music fits properly. Composers who use electronic keyboards where they do their composing can lay the SMPTE time code on a sophisticated recording machine and, with a video and sound track interlock system, actually complete a musical score by recording electronic music in sync with the video. This method eliminates the need for a music editor or an orchestra.

· 4 ·

Prescore

THE ADVANTAGES OF A PRESCORE

Any production in which at least five musical numbers or scenes are an integral part of the script is qualified to be referenced as a musical by the Academy of Motion Picture Arts and Sciences. The classic musical, such as *My Fair Lady, Music Man, Evita, Oklahoma, Camelot, West Side Story,* is a true rarity for today's moviegoer. The productions that qualify as musicals by today's standards are those in which five or more original songs are all written by the same writer or group of writers and performed on screen. Because of the dearth of musicals, the Academy holds the Best Song Score award in abeyance unless there are enough entries to make a contest. However, the basic preparation for any musical remains a constant.

A creative direction and a complete understanding of the needs of a musical must emerge in the preproduction meetings. The more definitive and meticulous the planning, the more smoothly the production will flow. These preproduction planning sessions give a sense of the complexity of a project and foster admiration for the individuals who have the internal fortitude to attempt to bring all the elements together to make a film or video production, and also for the interdependency and expertise of all the craftspeople who contribute.

In the first preproduction planning session, the director will give the set designer his or her thoughts on the staging of the music numbers, the furniture needed, the background settings, and the stage ambience. The choreographer will discuss the number of dancers, the costumes, and his or her visualization of a routine based on the director's staging. The composer will focus on the type of music, the length of each song, and the number of musicians and vocalists necessary for the various numbers. The producer will be on hand to maintain a sense of reality regarding the budget and the schedule,

The meetings that follow are to approve or modify the decisions made by each of the people involved and to work out the challenges presented by the schedule and, as always, the budget. Upon final approval of the songs and dance routines, preparations are made for the prescore.

The term *prescore* designates a recording session including an orchestra, musical group, instrument, or vocalist, made prior to the shooting of a musical scene.

The prescore may be recorded on the same stage that will be used later for recording the underscore music. However, because a prescore records music for a scene that has not yet been photographed, it follows that the music editor will not have any film or videotape to prepare; therefore, film or video projection facilities are not a necessity. A scoring stage or recording studio is reserved before the shooting, and musicians are booked to play on that session.

The composer will select a recording stage on the basis of the type of music and the number of musicians needed. The composer will instruct the music contractor as to the specific musicians that he or she would like to have play on that session, and the contractor will check the availability of those musicians and try to acquire their presence for that date.

To record any piece of music properly, several controls are necessary: (1) a soundproof room; (2) baffles to isolate the sounds of instruments in order to keep them from "swimming" together; (3) the placement of microphones to get the clearest, cleanest, most noise-free recording possible of each instrument; and (4) a mixing panel to control the volume and balance of individual instruments.

The sound quality of the music recorded on a shooting stage is never comparable to or as controllable as the quality of sound recorded under the quality control of a scoring stage. A prescore session enables the composer or conductor to rehearse, perfect, and then record a piece of music under ideally controllable conditions. If a vocal is to be part of the musical number, the most common procedure is to record the instrumental arrangement first and then call the vocalist. When the conductor is satisfied with the musicians' performances and the music has been recorded, the orchestra can be dismissed. Then the vocalist, while listening to the instrumental recording through headphones, can record onto the tracks saved for that purpose on a multitrack tape recording machine. In this relaxed atmosphere, the composer can concentrate on the nuances, shadings, and inflections of the vocal rendition.

When both the vocal and the instrumental must be recorded at the same time, the vocalist is placed in an isolation booth, while again listening to the orchestra through headphones. In either case, this ensures a vocal track that is isolated from the orchestra. This isolation is important to allow separation of the volume control of the vocal from that of the instruments.

The complexity or simplicity of the material to be prescored has a direct bearing on the question of who will preside over the prescore session. A composer might be on hand to supervise and conduct, and a music editor will always be present to log the takes and ensure that the music is transferred properly. If the music to be recorded is a single instrument or a small group that will be performing for "source tunes" (such as music emanating from a radio, television, or Muzak), then it is possible that the music editor could be the only production person supervising and conducting the prescore recording.

A prescore session can be as simple as a musician playing a solo, or as complex as a large Busby Berkeley–style musical number. One some occasions a playback will contain only a piano guide track, prerecorded for a sequence, which will be enhanced later by a full orchestra on the postproduction underscore session. This saves the cost of calling an orchestra for a prescore session in cases where they will surely be needed for the full score later. It can include augmenting the piano prescore track at that time.

As the scope of the prescore music increases, the number of production people with a vested interest in the prescore grows. They include the executive producer, director, line producer, associate producer, composer, choreographer, vocalist, and music supervisor, all of whom could be present to observe and give their input on the prescore stage. Each musical sequence is analyzed individually; although some similarities may exist, approaches, execution, and adjustments will be unique for each project.

When an arrangment of a standard tune, a popular tune, or an original piece of music is required for the sequence, then a composer or arranger is needed to conduct the session.

For a large prescore, a composer, orchestrator, contractor, copyist, and librarian will all be present, as they will for a postproduction underscore.

PRESCORE FOR DANCE ROUTINES

When a musical has dance sequences, a choreographer and a composer are an integral part of the preproduction meetings. The overall planning is the same whether the musical material is original for the production or consists of well-known tunes. The director, choreographer, and composer will work with the set designer in staging the musical numbers and determining the number of musicians needed, the instrumentation, the type of arrangement, and the tempo. Once the choreographer and the composer have a good mental picture of how the director wants to interpret the scene, the two work very closely together. All this preparatory work will result in a prescore session.

When a musical dance number is prescored, the choreographer will work with the composer both before the prescore session and on the prescore stage to lay out and perfect the musical arrangement and the timing of the dance routine. The dance steps or taps can also be recorded along with the prescore music or can be duplicated at a later time on the Foley stage. On a Foley stage, the film or video is projected on a screen, and Foley walkers duplicate the footsteps and movement of the actors in the picture in a controlled environment. In this instance professional dancers would be brought in to duplicate the dance routine.

The decision to record the taps is based on the performing

actor's ability to duplicate the steps exactly as the choreographer performed them on the prescored dance track. When the dance steps are included with the prescore, the on-screen shooting of the sequence has no room for error, and the performer must match the dance steps exactly.

LOCATION PRESCORING

A prescore is necessary because of the complexity of recording music on a production shooting stage. The quarter-inch recording machine on the shooting set is used primarily to record dialogue. On the rare occasions when music does have to be recorded on location, the set recordist will attempt to find a location as noise-free as possible to record the prescore.

If ethnic music or indigenous musicians are needed for authenticity on a location shoot, a prescore will be recorded on or near the shooting set. This occurs most often when a local choral group or marching band is to be part of the scene. If a parade is going to take place, a complete rendition of the tune the marching band is going to play should be prerecorded before the scene is shot. The recordist can set up and record a clean sound when there is no concern about microphones visibly interfering with the camera framing. (A second Nagra recorder will play back the prescored music when the time comes to photograph the band.) This type of recording is logged on the recordist's log as "wild" (camera not rolling). If there is a good prescore recording, then the director and the editor will have no concern regarding matching pickups, metric consistency, or bad playing during the filming that would necessitate a reshoot or pickups for the musicians. This gives everyone the assurance that the musicians will sound their very best regardless of what happens when the scene is photographed.

PRESCORE DUB DOWN

The music recorded on the prescore stage will have been recorded directly onto either a half-inch four-track tape, or a larger-capacity tape. There are 16-, 24-. 32-, and 48-track recording machines available, and when one of these is used, it necessitates a dub down to a half-inch four-track tape. (*Dub down* is the mixing or blending of many tracks into fewer.) This dub down to a half-inch four-track tape for playback could have a very basic format. The entire orchestration is assigned to track 1, leaving tracks 2 and 3 vacant, with the sync or SMPTE pulse on the fourth channel.

If the desired end product is stereo, then the mix for the orchestra could be on tracks 1 and 3, with the vocal or lead instrument in the center channel. Many times there will be two half-inch tapes needed in the dub downs. The orchestra is separated into three sections: track 1 with the strings, track 2 with the brass, and track 3 with the percussion. The second half-inch tape will contain the vocal on the first channel and a composite or complete orchestra mix on the third track. The orchestra on the first tape will be saved on 35 mm three-channel full-coat for the final dubbing or sweetening session. The composite orchestra and vocal on the second half-inch tape will be transferred to 35 mm full-coat three channel film, and both will be referred to as the *35 master*. It is from the 35 mm full-coat master with the vocal that the quarter-inch stage playbacks are made.

A sync pulse or SMPTE time code is not necessary on any magnetic film that is sprocketed. The sprocket holes on the 35 master will negate slippage, and all 35 mm sound track reproducers maintain a consistent speed.

A PRIMER OF MUSIC TERMS
FOR FILM AND VIDEO

Before proceeding into the more technical realm of music preparation, for the uninitiated person who will be dealing with composers and music in a pragmatic matter, it is necessary to understand the terms that are in constant use.

You do not need to be a musician to understand the process of blending music and film or video. Composers are trained to create the music and manage the more purely musical problems posed by the production process. However, many other people will be involved with the composers and the music itself, and they can benefit from understanding some basic music concepts.

What follows is a little of the language of music. It may help you communicate better with others involved in the production. These descriptions are not meant to be comprehensive, but they do cover the basics.

Music is essentially structured sound. Different cultures have developed their own standard systems to enable people to appreciate this structured sound. Thus, in many ways music is truly a language.

Bar   On the staff, a vertical line designating the end of a measure.
Beat   An accented point in music.

Chord   Three or more tones played simultaneously, which ideally complement each other and create a coherent effect.

Harmony   Multiple strains or sequences of notes played simultaneously. Successful harmony blends the different strains so that they reinforce one another and the melody, creating a richer sound than one strain alone would make possible.

Key   A system of musical tones defined in relation to one another, in a sense the "key" to understanding the composition of the piece of music.

Measure   A music unit defined by a certain number of beats contained in a bar.
Melody   The most recognizable of all the strains of music within a composition.
Meter   The number of beats in a bar and their time value.

Note   The written representation of a tone. Different notes may also have different durations and emphases.

Part   Sequences of notes intended to be played by a particular type of instrument.
Pitch   A primary quality of a tone, determined by its frequency, the number of sound vibrations per unit of time.

Rest   A music pause in which no note is played, but the musician literally rests the number of beats indicated.
Rhythm   A definable pattern of stressed beats.

Scale   A progressive, ordered sequence of tones.

Score   Music composed for enhancing the emotional impact of visual scenes. To create a musical composition. A musical score is the composition in written form, including all the various strains and parts.

Staff   (also called a *bar chart* or *bar graph*) A graph composed of five horizontal lines on which music is written. Notes are written to be read and played from left to right across the length of the staff; higher and lower notes appear, respectively, higher and lower on the staff. Notes in an ascending scale move progressively up the staff.

Tempo   The pace of a performed piece of music.

Time   A term generally describing the speed and rhythm of a piece of music. For example, *4/4 time* indicates that there are four beats per measure and that a quarter note (a note of a particular relative duration) is assigned one full beat.

Tone   A basic unit of music representing a definable sound.

Tune   To adjust an instrument to achieve its appropriate pitch. Various instruments playing in ensemble may need to be tuned to a stable reference source.

When writing a piece of music, a composer can create any number of parts for particular types of instruments, but there are a standard number of parts for a full orchestra. These correspond to the primary sections of an orchestra: strings (violins, violas, cellos, string basses), woodwinds (flutes, clarinets, oboes), brass (trumpets, trombones, french horns), and percussion (drums, cymbals, timpani). Generally, the concertmaster is the leader of the string section, who acts as an assistant to the conductor.

· 5 ·

Playbacks

UNDERSTANDING PLAYBACKS

A *playback* is the prescored music, properly prepared and transferred to quarter-inch tape, to be broadcast on the shooting set from a sound reproducer. Although many types of tape recorders have been created for a wide range of uses, the portable recorders manufactured by Nagra Magnetic Recorders, Inc., are among the best in quality and have become almost standard equipment for film and video productions. If you use a recorder to play back music or record any sound on a set, chances are it will be a Nagra.

The prescore recording session is dubbed down to a quarter-inch four-channel tape and then transferred to a 35 mm full-coat, referred to as the master. Before the 35 master is sent to make the quarter-inch stage playback tape, if the percussionist on the session did not give a vocal count-off or rim shots to the *down beat*, then some *in tempo* warning beeps are cut in or taped onto this track by the music editor. These beeps set a tempo for the first note of music, or to the down beat of the first *bar*. When a count-off or beeps are included, then the 35 master is properly prepared to make the quarter-inch stage playback tape. The request to the sound transfer department reads as follows: "From the submitted 35 full-coat three-channel, please make two composite quarter-inch tapes with sync pulse, small reels, 7½ IPS [inches per second] for stage play-back." The second tape is a protection copy in the event the first one is damaged or misplaced. Upon completion of the transfer operation, audio cassettes are ordered from this quarter-inch play-back tape and are given to the actors and musicians for rehearsal and familiarization.

How many times have you seen actors playing a piano or vocalizing on screen and wondered whether they were really play-ing that instrument or singing that song? The odds are better than ten to one that the instrument or vocal of the song you heard was prescored and a playback was used. That does not mean that it is not the actor's voice or that the actor did not play the instrument; it means only that the actor may or may not have been the one who recorded on the prescore session. A professional musician or vocal-ist may have done the recording, and the actor may then have mimed the playing or singing on camera.

PLAYBACKS ON PRODUCTION

On the shooting set there are three people involved with sound: a *production mixer* who operates the quarter-inch Nagra recorder and is totally responsible for the sound, a *boom person* who positions and manipulates the microphone, and a *cable puller* who assists the boom person. When the scheduled day arrives to photograph the musical sequence, the production manager will have requested a playback sound operator and the proper synchro-nous Nagra tape machine with a speaker system. The playback operator will have placed the playback tape in position on the Nagra so the count-off or beeps are the first thing heard. The camera person calls, "Rolling," the sound person calls, "Speed," and the director calls "Action," after which he or she indicates either vocally or with a hand signal that the playback should start. The introductory count-off or beeps cue the actors for the start of the music. The principals should duplicate the playback by playing the instruments and singing aloud, as the recorded production track will later be replaced with the 35 mm master playback track.

If there is any noticeable deviation in the playing of instruments or an inconsistency in the lip sync of the vocalist to the playback, the director will have instructed the music editor either to stop the take or to make a note that at a particular point the performers went out of sync with the playback. When this situation occurs, the director will make a value judgment whether to reshoot the entire scene or to shoot just the part of the scene where the error was made. The latter procedure is referred to as a *pickup*. A pickup is requested when, within a take, an actor has flubbed a line and, rather than reshooting the entire scene, just that phrase is reshot to perfect that section. A pickup is applicable to any scene, musical or not, shot on a set. In the case of a music playback, the musicians on the set must duplicate the exact motions of the prerecorded playback and the vocalist must duplicate the lip movements. If there has been an inconsistency in shooting the scene, and the director opts for a pickup, the music editor listens to the quarter-inch playback tape and inserts a start mark, either a stick-on tab or a white grease pencil mark, a few bars before the musical phrase that is to be picked up. This is referred to as an *internal start*. Any number of internal starts can be improvised as shooting progresses, or the quarter-inch tape can be preprogrammed by the director and choreographer before the shooting of the sequence.

On occasion, when a playback is used for a long production dance routine, the music editor will use one channel of a stereo quarter-inch Nagra track to record a vocal count of bars or sections. This vocal count can be played simultaneously with the playback music or used only to locate a section.

When shooting to a playback, you do not have to concern yourself with microphone placement, room ambience, stage noises, or the musicians' playing and vocal performance. All these contingencies are dealt with under the ideal conditions of the prescore stage.

Annie, Yentl, and most other music song scores were shot entirely to playbacks. It would be financially prohibitive to have a full orchestra, on or off camera, playing for the vocals and dance routines of such a musical extravaganza. The production sound mixer, attempting to record the full orchestra and the vocalist, with all the movement inherent to a choreographed number, would find it impossible to get a clean, usable music track.

Playbacks are almost mandatory when shooting a musical sequence with either film or videotape. If the musical scene to be photographed has a single instrument or even a small group, a monaural playback is fine. When there is a vocalist with the group, then the possibility of using two channels (stereo Nagra) should be considered.

NAGRA RECORDERS

There are two types of quarter-inch tape machines: a monaural recorder and a stereo recorder. A monaural Nagra will carry the sync pulse or SMPTE time code on a side channel of the tape and the playback material on another. A stereo Nagra reads the sync pulse in the center of the tape and has two channels available for recording and/or playback. The quarter-inch Nagra monaural recorder and the stereo recorder machines are not interchangeable.

Will you want a playback with a monaural quarter-inch 60-cycle sync pulse for the playback? Do you think a stereo with vocal on one track and instruments on the other will serve you better? You must decide which one to use before ordering the playback tape, as compatible equipment will be necessary to reproduce the recorded sound on the set. The advantage of a two-track stereo tape for playback lies in the individual volume control of each of the channels. One speaker can be positioned for the performing musicians and the other for the vocalist. When the camera is on the vocalist, the vocal channel can be increased in volume without raising the volume of the instrumental group. Conversely, when a close-up of the performing musicians is being filmed, the volume of the instrumental channel can be raised and the vocal held down. This type of control aids the artists with their synchronization, for in most cases the musicians who recorded the playback music will not be the ones performing on the set, and the isolated instrumental channel will enable the actors to hear and duplicate the performance of the recording musicians more easily.

PLAYBACKS FOR DANCE ROUTINES

There is an interesting difference between the *metric* counting of the bars for musicians and that for dancers. Musicians count bars and beats in 4/4 time as follows: (bar one) *1*-2-3-4, (bar two) *2*-2-3-4, (bar three) *3*-2-3-4, and so on. Choreographers and dancers, however, count in two-bar phrases. The count in 4/4 time from the first bar to the downbeat of the fifth reads *A*-2-3-4-5-6-7-8, *B*-2-3-4-5-6-7-8, *C* (downbeat of the fifth), and so on. This count is necessitated by the fact that dance routines are choreographed in eight-beat steps. Substituting sequential letters for bar numbers for the first beat of a two-bar phase also provides an easy identification on the playback tape to ensure the proper internal starts for different sections of the piece.

SPEAKER SYSTEMS

An alternative to the standard speaker system that broadcasts the playback over the complete set is an *earwig*, a small receiver, shaped in the form of a hearing aid, that fits into the ear. The earwig merely replaces the speakers; the Nagra tape player and the playback operator will function in the same manner. The shooting area on the set must be completely encircled by an antenna wire that can be placed either overhead or on the floor. All those standing within the circle will hear the playback through their earwigs.

An example of the effectiveness of the earwig is seen in a film like *My Fair Lady*. Professor Higgins, hearing the orchestra through his earwig, could deliver his semispoken, semisung lines in pitch and tempo to the prerecorded playback music. The production mixer, using the earwig system, can record a clean vocal track without the broadcast sound of the playback speakers on the set. The earwig is also invaluable when a choir or group is singing. The on-camera conductor or leader will have the earwig to aid in keeping the proper pitch and meter.

On the other hand, prescored vocals, in which lip sync is so important, and large musical production numbers, in which dancers must be in meter, will use the conventional playback system.

The most challenging aspect of planning musical setups is that there are very few absolutes. No two scenes are exactly alike, and every situation has its own unique definitive guidelines.

METRONOME PLAYBACKS

Metronomes are mechanical or electronic devices that help performers maintain a tempo by supplying a regular beat. Although metronomes are used extensively in postproduction scoring sessions, they can also be used during production playbacks.

There are metronome beat playbacks that, when broadcast on the shooting set to keep a ballroom dance scene in tempo, have such a low frequency that the clicks or beats can be filtered out of the set recorder's track without affecting the recorded dialogue.

SOURCE MUSIC FOR PLAYBACKS

The most commonly used and most abused practice is that of playing commercial records or audio cassettes as source music. To avoid the extra expense of calling a playback operator and renting a Nagra recorder with a speaker system, a record or an audio cassette may be broadcast on the set when music is needed for a ballroom dance scene. Neither a commercial record nor a cassette can ever be an exact match when transferred to 35 mm magnetic film, the necessary format for the final dub.

The preproduction meeting should include a discussion and a decision concerning the selection of music for the ballroom scene. Then, a sync license for the tune should be acquired. A sync license indicates that the production company has paid for the rights to use a published song in a film or video production. The recording company should be contacted to supply the production company with a quarter-inch stereo tape copy of the recording, rather than transferring from a record or cassette. This quarter-inch tape will not have a sync pulse or SMPTE time code; therefore, the first step in the operation is to get this recording onto sprocketed film.

A transfer of the supplied quarter-inch, from record or cassette, is made to a 35 mm full-coat magnetic film with a stereo format on two of the three available tracks. This 35 full-coat is now the master, and a quarter-inch tape with a sync pulse and warning beeps will be made for the stage playback from this master. When this procedure is followed, thereafter, any prints transferred for the picture editor or music editor will always be in perfect sync.

The exception to this rule came with the advent of compact discs (CDs). Because CDs are formatted digitally, they have no variance in speed, regardless of the machine on which they are played. They are always consistent in time. This exception does not preclude following the same procedure in making a 35 mm master from that CD, inserting the warning beeps, and then transferring the master to the quarter-inch tape for stage playback.

CODING PLAYBACKS

Every *take* of a musical sequence using a playback is recorded by the production mixer. Because these takes contain the broadcast of the playback over the speakers as well as the sounds of the performers either singing or faking the playing of instruments, they cannot be used in the final dub. These production tracks containing the sound of the playback are referred to as *scratch tracks* and are used by the music editor as a guide to sync the original 35 master playback track with the picture.

The 35 master is assigned and edge-numbered with a special music code that places a consecutive inked number along the edge on every foot of the 35 master. Every picture angle of the dailies that contains the music from the playback, in addition to the normal daily code assigned by the assistant picture editor, is again coded identically with the music code numbers that appear on the 35 master. Another transfer from the 35 master to a single-stripe track with this duplicated number is delivered to the picture editor. This track will replace the playback section of the scratch tracks. By lining up the music codes on the picture dailies or rushes with the code on the music track, no matter what angle is being cut, the picture will always be in perfect sync with the music.

· 6 ·

Live Recording
on the Set

CHALLENGES OF LIVE RECORDING

On the production set, when a musical instrument or vocal is going
to be recorded live, a consultation with a knowledgeable composer,
music supervisor, or music editor is of the utmost importance. The
most insignificant improvisation of any type of music—an actor
whistling a song, humming a tune, strumming a guitar, or playing
any other musical instrument—requires the attention of a music
supervisor. Take a simple scene in which an actor strums a guitar.
It would seem ridiculous to be concerned about a possible compli-
cation, but if the composer has to underscore this scene later, that
guitar chord or chords will need to be in proper pitch. Before any
music is strummed or played in the scene, it is necessary that it be
in tune.

When a tune is being sung, hummed, or whistled, it is very
important that it be in proper pitch. If there are pickups to be made
or different angles to be shot, a music supervisor with a pitch pipe
should be on the shooting set to give the actor the proper pitch of
the first note of the tune, and a metronome should be used to give
and maintain a consistent tempo each time the tune has to be

repeated. In some cases, the music supervisor will hold rehearsals with the actor or actors and possibly conduct off camera while the scene is being shot. Tempo and pitch consistency enable the picture or video editor to intercut close-up shots with a master shot or two-shot that otherwise would not match because of a discordant change in pitch and tempo.

A good example would be a scene of children singing "Row, Row, Row Your Boat" in a bus. The director plans to shoot the scene with one angle covering the teacher conducting in the front of the bus, then a reverse angle favoring the children, and then a final angle with close-ups of individual children. Each time, the actors sing the entire song, or at least that part of the song that will be intercut.

The opening shot of the teacher conducting goes smoothly and is a print. The camera, which was shooting from the back of the bus, now must be repositioned for the next shot of the group singing. All the participants have to get out of the bus or, worse, hold their positions for lighting while the crew moves forward to set up the new angle. Finally, an hour later, they are ready to shoot the reverse over-shoulder angle of the teacher conducting. The director calls, "Action," and the children again start singing "Row, Row, Row Your Boat." The actor who plays the part of the teacher is not facing the camera in this angle; consequently, her energy level has lessened and her conducting is a bit slower. Next, the camera is repositioned for the children's close-ups. With the camera lens right in their faces, they are more self-conscious; they sing the song faster and in a higher key.

When the picture editor attempts to intercut this material, there is a terrible mismatch because the three angles are all different in tempo and pitch. The out-of-pitch singing can be corrected by an electronic device called a *harmonizer*, which will change the pitch without changing the speed of the singing. Nothing can be done about the change of tempo; the picture editor will have to do some creative editing to remedy this problem.

In this example there is a choice: playback or live. The scene could be shot to a playback, but in the process the director might lose the spontaneity of the children. The answer might be to shoot the scene live, with musical supervision, or to use a simple piano playback track with an earwig for the teacher to act as a guide while she is singing and conducting the children. A music consultant could be on the set with a pitch pipe and a metronome to keep everyone rhythmically correct and in tune.

SIMPLE LIVE RECORDING—VOCALS

To take a more basic example, suppose the scene calls for an actress to enter an office, humming a tune as she enters, crossing the room, and seating herself at a desk.

Before any concrete decision is made about what tune will be hummed, a group of acceptable tune titles should be gathered and a music clearance house contacted to get the usage fees for the different melodies. Once the cost of the tunes is known, a decision can be made about which tune to use, and the production office can incorporate the cost into the music budget.

The director requests a full shot of the actor entering and crossing the room, and a second, closer angle of the actor seating herself while reacting to a piece of mail on the desk. A music supervisor with a pitch pipe sounds a starting note for her to begin humming and, while listening to the beat of a pocket-sized metronome, establishes the proper tempo ensuring a consistency for each scene shot. The music supervisor notes the phrase in the tune at which the actor starts to seat herself at the desk, so the close-up shot angle can begin with the same phrase of the tune. This enables the editor to make a smooth musical transition when integrating the full shot and the close-up angle. This method works with any vocal rendition, either on location or on a sound stage.

LIVE RECORDING—MUSIC

The decision to shoot live music on the set presents a different set of challenges to the production mixer. The mixer knows the proper placement for the microphone to achieve the best sound recording but is seldom able to exercise that expertise. On the shooting set, everything is positioned for the camera; neither the mixer's microphone nor its shadow is allowed to be seen within the camera's framing. (It's as if Michelangelo were commissioned to paint a mural on the Sistine Chapel but had to work from the floor using a hundred-foot-long paintbrush.) This, however, is all a part of the production mixer's job.

Let's take as an example a scene requiring a recording of an actor playing a guitar. To record this instrument properly, the microphone should be placed about two feet away from the guitar's sounding board. Unfortunately, that would put the microphone within the camera's framing, so the boom person has to hold the microphone overhead, six feet away from the guitar. Because the shooting set has none of the acoustic qualities or sound baffles that are needed for control, the production mixer will be picking up the sound of the guitar and also all the room ambience. In the final dub, if the volume is to be raised on the guitar, all of the room ambience will also increase. This is not an ideal condition, but everything needed to record the guitar is available on the set.

If the scene requires the actor to sing and play the guitar simultaneously, the lack of control intensifies because the vocal and the guitar will be locked together on the same track. Alternatives do exist. The Nagra used by the production mixer has one channel for recording, and the other uses a sync pulse. A stereo Nagra can be ordered that would allow the production mixer to use one microphone for the guitar and another microphone for the vocal. The guitar and vocal will have separate tracks, with the center channel carrying the sync pulse. Because the actor will be playing and singing at the same time, there will be leakage in both tracks. The top track, recording the vocal, will also pick up the sound of the guitar; conversely, the guitar track will also pick up the vocal. This presupposes that the scene would visually allow for this type of microphone setup. If the recording is satisfactory, then it will go into the production as planned. If not, the vocal and the guitar will have to be rerecorded separately for volume control in the postproduction phase.

If you have a trio and want to use three microphones, the production mixer would order a half-inch four-track machine that provides three tracks to use for recording, with the fourth track for the sync pulse. The mixer will also need a sound-mixing panel with four-channel control to accommodate such an assignment. As the size of the group increases, the number of microphones needed increases, as does the size of the recording equipment.

The next step up is to a one-inch eight-track recorder, with seven tracks available to the mixer and the eighth track used for a sync pulse or SMPTE. This necessitates an even larger recording panel and, ideally, the addition of a music mixer to the sound recording crew. If a full orchestra or concert is to be recorded, then we move up to a 24-, 32- or 48-track recording machine. Now, in addition to the production mixer, a music mixer is needed to supervise the microphone setup and to record the music. The music mixer, mixing panel, and recording equipment are usually located in a mobile sound trailer.

The production mixer will have placed the microphone for the on-set recording in the best location to record the overall sound of the music and, if applicable, the audience reaction. The music mixer in the sound trailer attempts to record something as close to a scoring stage mix as possible. The music mixer will have as many microphones as possible placed in front of either individual instruments or instrumental sections. In this circumstance, the recording made by the production mixer with the overall microphone will be of great value in maintaining the authenticity of the crowd reactions. In most cases this track will be usable for the crowd reactions, as the music mixer's recording will overshadow the set recorder's track and they may be able to play simultaneously when the final dub is made.

The Buddy Holly Story is a prime example of a live shoot in which every musical number was recorded live on the set. The concert was photographed with all the excitement of audience participation, which would have been impossible to achieve with a playback. The energy generated by a live audience gives musicians and performers an enthusiasm that is reflected in their playing. These are hectic sessions when recording a concert, and everything that can possibly go wrong will. But, careful preplanning can help to eliminate the most obvious pitfalls.

· 7 ·

The Composer

SELECTING A COMPOSER

It is advantageous for a producer to select and contractually com-
mit a composer to a project in the preproduction stage. This
ensures his or her availability for consultation purposes and re-
serves the composer's time when the project is ready to be underscored. The producer is usually the dominant decision maker in the
selection of a composer. She should take into consideration the
individual talent, temperament, and idiosyncrasies of a composer
in deciding who would be best to score the production. Composers
have their specialties; some are more comfortable with a romantic
drama than they would be with an action or horror picture.

Good composers recognize their limitations in deference to the
writing of different styles and moods of music. Other issues may be
important to them. Some would not consider working on a film
that glorifies violence, carries a message with which they disagree,
or is offensive to them for personal reasons. For example, on one
project three composers individually turned down an opportunity
to compose music for a film in which each felt a dictator was
portrayed in too favorable a light.

There are a few composers with such musical stature and reputation that producers rely on them completely for their taste and discretion. The producer must be aware of the composer's style and should know beforehand the quality (and expense) of acquiring this composer's talents.

On occasion, the producer is superseded by a director whose contract stipulates a specific composer for any film or video project he directs or grants the director power of choice.

READING THE SCRIPT

When a producer buys or is assigned a script, she will carefully analyze every scene for the most economical means to shoot that script while staying within budgetary limitations. If there are musical sequences, a composer will be engaged to read the script and estimate the number of musicians needed and the amount of prescore time necessary to accommodate those sequences. On some occasions the producer will send a script to a composer, even though it has no musical sequences, to ascertain if he would be interested in working on the project. All these are valid reasons for a composer to read a script.

There are some definite disadvantages of a composer's having read a script before seeing the completed production. The script will give the composer information that will affect his emotional responses when he is called in to view the final cut. The emotions he feels in response to the picture will be drastically curtailed because, having read the script, the composer knows what is going to happen. Invariably, after the screening, the producer or director will ask the composer something like, "When did you first have the feeling that the butler did it?" Of course, the honest answer will be, "Three months ago, when I first read the script."

In reading a script, the reader conceives mental images of how he feels the scene should be played. Thus, the picture on the screen, having been interpreted by the director and limited by the producer's budget, will have an intellectual rather than an emotional impact on the viewer. The disappointment that comes from reading a good book and then seeing a motion picture of that story is a good example. The film never lives up to the mental images that have been created by the reader. In film and video making, there is a strong possibility that reading the script will have an adverse influence on the composer's musical underscoring of the picture. Just as the original script has been meticulously studied and changes have been made to accommodate the idiosyncrasies of the actors, so there will also be budget limitations affecting the locale and sets. These changes, in turn, will have an influence on the original script. There will also be improvisations on a shooting set that give nuances that do not appear on the written page. Under the director's influence, personal emotions that the shooting script elicits from the reader could be lost or enhanced above the reader's expectations. The only time a viewer can be emotionally objective in evaluating a production is the first time he sees the picture—and only if he hasn't first read the script.

The bottom line is that in most cases the composer should read the script before seeing the picture only if it is essential to the production.

THE COMPOSER ON LOCATION

In many instances, it behooves the producer to include the composer on a production location to absorb the ethnic music and the expertise (or lack of it) of the musicians in that locale. The composer can achieve authenticity by recording indigenous musical groups for source music, and this ethnic music may have a strong influence on the composer in composing the final score. Under these circumstances, the composer is considered an integral part of the production and can be placed on salary (usually, composers contract for a flat fee) and restricted from working on any other project until the final score is complete. This type of total commitment for the composer certainly does not represent the norm. But this arrangement gives the composer an opportunity to become intimately involved with the mood and dynamics of the film.

THE COMPOSER
IN POSTPRODUCTION

In the postproduction phase, music becomes a major interest of the producer and director. Up to this point, all efforts and creativity have been concentrated on production values and editing. Now, as the film or video is in complete assembly, the value of music in enhancing the emotions of scenes comes to the forefront.

With the majority of films and television productions, the composer will not become involved until the picture is in the final editing stages. The producer usually will contact a composer with whom she has worked successfully in the past, or with some of whose recent scores she is familiar. The producer wants and needs a composer who she feels will make a real contribution to her production.

A composer will be invited to view an assembly or rough cut. The *rough cut* is the first assembly before the project has been polished and brought down to the proper running time. After this screening, the producer and/or director will exchange general information with the composer regarding the type and style of music needed and the approach to follow. She might tell the composer the direction and flavor the music should take—for example, ethnic instruments with a lot of tension and low strings, not too melodic, but not too heavy either; or a tense, pulsating electronic score. It is at this time that the composer will decide if her thoughts are compatible and if she will be able to accommodate the producer's or director's musical interpretations.

A short time later (one hopes), the picture will be in final cut. A spotting session can then be scheduled, during which the placement, length, and general type of underscore is determined. No definitive music can be written until after the spotting session. The interim between viewing the original rough cut and the official spotting session of the final cut gives the composer time for musical research, working on a theme, or writing any general source music.

THE SPOTTING SESSION

A spotting session is scheduled with the producer, director, picture editor, and composer, along with a music editor, to select scenes and areas to be underscored. The spotting session takes place in a screening room or in the film or videotape editor's cutting or assembly room. The screening facility should be able to play the picture both forward and in reverse, allowing those present to pinpoint the exact dialogue or action where each segment of music should begin and end. Each segment of required music is termed a *music cue* and is given a number by reel and location within that reel.

When film is being run in a projection room, there is a footage counter immediately below the screen that will start at 000 for the beginning of each reel. When screening a video production, the visual time code replaces the need for a counter. The music editor makes a note of the footage or time code numbers at which the producer, director, and composer have agreed the music should start and stop. The note will also include a brief description of the scene and pertinent comments made by the producer, director, and composer regarding the tempo, meter, instrumentation, and specific accents or changes in mood. See Chapter 8 for more detail on spotting notes.

Artistic control or decision making in a spotting session varies from one project to the next. In some instances the producer will be in charge, but more often it will be the director. Regardless of the line of authority, it must be a collaborative effort. Discussion prevails as to the validity and emotional need to underscore given scenes. This is not to negate the composer's influence in the spotting session, but rather to list those with whom he has to share the honor of spotting the production.

The integration of music—where it will color, accentuate, or intensify the emotional content—is a sensitive and delicate decision. There are no rules, no guidelines; the only criteria are the emotions felt when screening the production.

People have their own individual emotional responses to any given scene, and therefore a spotting session affords a variety of opinions. The producer or director may request a musical theme for every principal actor, whereas others will be more concerned with mood than with specific thematic material. Producers and directors who have had difficulties in dealing with an actor during a production may allow their personal feelings to interfere with their judgment—for example, by asking that music be played under every scene in which that actor appears. A composer who has not been privy to these production problems or personality conflicts can be more objective in a situation like this and be a better judge of the spotting of the music. Knowing where *not* to play music is as important as knowing where to play it.

Some producers and directors feel that if there isn't any dialogue, music should always fill the empty space. But in a quiet, lonely scene, if you add lonely music, you will diminish the feeling of emptiness by adding a foreign ingredient—music. Composers refer to this as "painting white on white." How can a composer be motivated to produce creative musical interpretations when the personal conviction is lacking?

The phrase producers and directors use in a spotting session to cover a lack of definitive instruction is, "Play against the scene." It is inherently difficult for anyone to describe, except in very general terms, the subtle musical qualities they feel are needed to underscore a scene.

It is the composer, in the isolation of the studio, who has to write the music. Without a personal conviction that a given scene should be underscored, he will lack the impetus and direction to make any kind of definitive emotional contribution. The underscore will be nothing more than "vanilla" or "fill" music.

Ideally, a composer will have a private screening with no one else present. This allows for total concentration, just sitting back and enjoying the picture. Then, after a few days of considering the musical possibilities, the composer should have another screening and spotting session, with a music editor making spotting notes. This system gives the composer a totally subjective spotting session and will give greater credence to his decisions when the producer and director are present for the official spotting session. The spotting notes are delivered to the composer, with copies to the producer and director. After they have had an opportunity to study these notes, a final spotting session is scheduled.

At this screening there is now a definitive outline for the music cues, and the producer and director can approve or disapprove of the composer's starts and stops.

This scenario would be the best of all possible worlds for the composer. In reality, however, time, schedules, and egos will, more often than not, preclude this arrangement.

At the completion of the spotting session, the music editor, who has been roughly timing each music cue's duration, will give the composer a rough estimate of the total duration of the music to be written. This amount of time will either relieve the composer, if the figure is low, or, if there is a lot of underscore, will send him cursing to his agent for getting him into such a mess.

RECORDING TIME

The music editor, from the rough notes taken during the spotting session, will time more exactly the cues, referring to a video or black-and-white dupe of the film. These exact timings and scene descriptions compose the *spotting notes*. The spotting notes list each of the music cues, giving the approximate total time and a brief description of each music selection. From these notes, the composer can determine how many minutes of music are to be recorded and, subsequently, how many hours of scheduled time will be required in the scoring stage. Let's say 42 minutes worth of music is required, and the composer knows that he will average 3 minutes of recorded music per hour in the scoring stage. Then 14 hours of recording time is needed. From the scene description, the composer can determine the size of the orchestra and how many musicians are needed to underscore any individual cue. Armed with this information, the composer first contacts a music contractor.

THE MUSIC CONTRACTOR

The music contractor helps select orchestra players for the composer. Orchestras can be broken down as follows: "A" orchestra (full complement of musicians), "B" orchestra (perhaps brass and percussion only), "C" orchestra (small group for source tunes), or any other musical combination dictated by the picture. The composer might categorize each cue as thematic, scenic, action, romance, emotional, tension, or source, and make further subdivisions among the themes.

Knowing that the total amount of music is to be 42 minutes and knowing how much time is needed for each orchestral group, the composer can determine the number of sessions. A rule of thumb is 3 minutes per hour for a feature; hence a three-hour session will average 9 minutes of recorded music. Therefore, to record all 42 minutes of music, there must be five three-hour sessions called. It might take two three-hour sessions to perfect a four-minute main title. Then the overall time must be balanced by increasing the amount of recorded music in the following sessions, with the easier, less complex cues.

Next, the composer, together with the contractor, selects the orchestra players best suited for this type of score. Is it to be an acoustic or an electronic score, or perhaps a combination of the two? When this decision is made, the music contractor will call the musicians to determine their availability for the scheduled scoring dates. If one or more of the desired musicians have prior commitments, then alternative players are called, or, in some instances, the scoring date will be changed to accommodate a particular musician's schedule. Perhaps the director or producer has specifically requested that the theme should feature a French horn, and the composer's favorite French horn player is not available for a specific date. In that case, the scoring session will be changed to accommodate the player's schedule.

Up to this point, the composer's activity consists mainly of organizational and thematic experimentation. The spotting notes contain overall timings, but the composer needs specific internal detailed timings of the action and dialogue within the music cue before any cue can be written.

When a composer receives a video cassette of a film or videotape program, it will have the SMPTE time code visually displayed on the picture. For a composer to calculate mathematically the inner timings of a cue would be a time-consuming exercise that has nothing to do with the creative act of writing music. One of the important functions of the music editor is to relieve the composer of this mathematical exercise. The music editor makes these calculations and provides the composer with exact timings in the form of *breakdown notes*.

WRITING THE SCORE

The composer will mark on the breakdown notes the timings at which musical accents or changes are wanted and then find a tempo that is comfortable for the scene.

Composers will not necessarily write a main title first. Some will start with the most complex or difficult cue—a long chase or a tender love cue—to see if an inspiration for a theme for the main title will evolve. There are as many options for where and how to start writing cues as there are composers.

Some composers orchestrate (arrange musical parts for an orchestra) their own compositions, whereas others delegate that work to an orchestrator. In the latter instance, the composer gives detailed sketches of the cues to an orchestrator who assigns the specific instrumental colors indicated on the composer's sketch into the full score. The completed orchestration of a sketch is referred to as the *score*. This score is given to a group of copyists, who write out the individual parts for each instrument.

For an average feature, the elapsed time from the spotting session to the scoring date will be four to six weeks. The amount of underscore music in a feature film will average around 50 minutes. A film scoring composer, writing 3 to 4 minutes of music per day, working a five-day week, will complete the music score in just under four weeks. This does not include research time, or the time it takes to reassure the producer and the director that the score is coming along nicely, or consultations with the music contractor and others involved with the project.

Schedules are tighter for a television "Movie of the Week," and the time allotted to the composer diminishes. The same amount (or more) of underscore music is needed for a two-hour television movie as for a feature film. But a composer is fortunate to be allowed three weeks to complete a score.

The writing time for episodic television is even shorter. The weekly episodes are written with much more facility, as the main title, end title, and bumper music consist of prerecorded material that is integrated into each episode by the music editor. The majority of the music cues to be written for the episode will be adapted from the main title theme. Nevertheless, episodic music composition turns into a frantic pressure cooker for composers and everyone involved in postproduction because of the tight scheduling.

This shortage of compositional time for a one-hour episodic television segment has a deleterious effect on composers. No composer can be expansive or give music a creative personalized touch under the time pressure exerted by the end-of-the-season rush. Working around the clock to meet an absolute deadline can be totally enervating. Music is one of the last elements to be added to a TV episode. At the beginning of the television season, the production office schedules enough time for everyone to do the job properly. As the season progresses, however, unexpected events will take place that cause inevitable changes in both the editing and the delivery dates. These originate from the strangest of circumstances—a sponsor requesting editing changes because a competitor's product is visually displayed in the film, or network executives being pressured by private-sector groups responding to sensitive material covered in the episode. Some of these requests come from so far afield that no one could possible have anticipated that anything in the picture would be offensive or unacceptable.

In episodic television, the main title theme is often used throughout the series (remember "Mission Impossible"?). The producer will instruct the composer to adapt the theme whenever the principals are working on camera. So much thematic material is used throughout many television series that the composer turns into an adapter. That is one reason episodic television can get by with such a tight schedule for composers to write the underscore. They do not have to write a great deal of original material but, rather, must adapt and improvise on the existing theme. The adaptation of a theme, of course, is not what composers most relish, unless they have written the theme.

When a composer writes an original piece of music for a film, she will receive credit for the composition on the music sync license form that is submitted to Broadcast Music Incorporated (BMI) or the American Society of Composers, Authors and Publishers (ASCAP), the two professional organizations supervising rights and royalties for music composers and publishers. If she adapts a piece of thematic material, credit goes to the composer who wrote the original theme. This represents a financial loss to the adapting composer and brings additional monies from domestic and foreign play to the original composer.

When the project is a feature picture, the producer may have purchased the rights to a song or a recording to be used over the main title. The composer is then requested to adapt that main title song for specific scenes throughout the film. This, again, is not usual and represents an additional expense for the production company, as the usage fee goes up each time the theme is reintroduced. This request for adaptation has the same effect on the feature composer as does the adaptation of the main title theme on the episodic television composer. In both instances, the composers are not writing original music and will receive no residual payments for foreign exhibition or domestic reruns.

ELECTRONICS

There was a time when the composer's only need in viewing a video cassette was to play an instrument while viewing the selected scene either to see how the music accommodated the section or to serve as a memory refresher. With the advent of electronic music, many composers have incorporated recording facilities in their home studios. With a three-quarter-inch video cassette with SMPTE time code on the second audio track, composers can "lock up" (synchronize) a multitrack tape recorder with the picture and score an entire film with a synclavier and other electronic instruments.

This has had a deleterious effect on many musicians' careers. Their calls have decreased as more and more composers are called on to furnish electronic scores. String players seem to be the most severely affected by this electronic invasion.

Many feature films will incorporate acoustic instruments and electronic sound, separately for some cues and recorded simultaneously for others. The unique electronic musical sounds now available to a composer are not to be denied. Composers are no longer kicking and screaming about the electronic invasion, but instead are experimenting and gaining new ground with this former nemesis.

THE LONELY COMPOSER

What ingredient comes to mind when one thinks of the makeup of a composer? A composer will look at a film in the final cut with the producer and director, and will view this picture with dialogue only. In the spotting session, along with the director and producer, he will have to pick the areas in the picture to be underscored. There must be a valid reason for every piece of underscore, and that underscore must enter unobtrusively, complement the scene, be original in content, and disappear as easily as it has entered.

The composer receives all the necessary notes and timings, and usually a video cassette of the picture as well. The only thing left is actually to write the music. He must create an original theme to set the mood of the picture, and this theme has to satisfy the director, producer, executive producer, and various heads of the studio or network. (Sometimes this elite group includes the ten-year-old daughter of one of the above.) The possible alternatives for themes and for orchestral or electronic arrangements are as varied as snowflakes in a blizzard.

No music has the ability to please everyone. It may soothe the savage breast in some and bring out unpleasant memories in others. These are the intangibles that the composer, to a greater or lesser degree, will have to face.

When the composer has to put notes on that empty score paper, there is no one there to hold his hand, make suggestions, or provide direction. He is on his own, for better or worse, laying out musically his personal emotional responses to each scene that is to be covered musically. Any criticism of the music can be interpreted as a personal attack, not only on his musical ability but also on his most private emotions.

One does not think of an artistic, sensitive composer as tough— after all, composers write beautiful, flowing, sensitive music—but tough is what they have to be. Their music exposes their talent, creativity, and sensitivity to all types of people, some of whom they may not even respect. The defenses that develop when one's emotions are constantly exposed will take many forms, and consequently there are many different personalities among composers.

There are some people who are in sympathy with the composer's position—the music editor, adapters, arrangers, orchestrators, possibly a spouse—but none of them have their own personal integrity exposed as the composer does.

But enough about the poor composer. Composers are fairly compensated for both the compliments and the complaints that arise from their work. Nevertheless, to say that it takes a very special kind of ego to undertake this most esoteric of endeavors is an understatement.

· 8 ·

The Music Editor

DUTIES OF THE MUSIC EDITOR

Upon completion of the spotting session for a project shot on film, the music editor will be supplied with a black-and-white dupe of the picture and a one-to-one of the track (a duplication of the editor's sound track). In the film productions, the music editor usually also receives a three-quarter-inch video. Obviously, in video productions the music editor receives only the video. With very few exceptions, a three-quarter-inch video cassette of the complete production will be used to make the spotting notes, breakdown notes, and bar charts (score paper indicating beats with information about what is taking place on those beats), and to put streamers and clicks on the video for the scoring stage.

TIMING TO FILM

Before the advent of videotape, the music editor would do all of the music spotting and breakdown notes, streamering of the picture for projection on the scoring stage, and building of the music dubbing units using the black-and-white dupe picture and track. The dupe picture and track were threaded on a moviola equipped with a seconds counter (film runs at 24 frames per second), in addition to the standard footage counter showing feet and frames (16 frames per foot). The film was run down to the frame where the music was to start. The footage and frame were noted and the seconds counter was set to 00:00.0. As the scene played, every action was described, and each line of dialogue, both the start and the end of each phrase, was timed from the seconds counter. This operation is still used by music editors who are not equipped with video facilities.

TIMING TO VIDEO

When a video cassette is used to time the breakdown notes, the music editor must have a three-quarter-inch video cassette player with a manual control that permits easy location of any frame desired and, of course, a video monitor. The music editor will use the three-quarter-inch video cassette to give a precise description and accurate timing of the scenes that have been spotted. The videotape program must have been ordered with a visible SMPTE time code displayed in the window of each frame indicating the hour, minute, second, and frame number, in addition to the identical SMPTE time code included on the second audio and also on the address track.

The video is run down to the frame indicated at the spotting session, and the SMPTE time code number of that frame will be noted on the breakdown sheet, for example :00.09:21:18, indicating 0 hours, 9 minutes, 21 seconds, and 18 frames (video has 30 frames per second). As the scene plays, the SMPTE numbers increase in time and frame count. Consequently, to determine the inner timing of any action, the *start time count* must be subtracted from the time and frame count at the end of the scene being timed to establish the actual time lapse. Videotape registers 30 frames per second, and the frame count numbers must be converted to tenths of seconds.

The conversion of video frames to tenths of seconds should not split the difference but should always err so that the music timing falls either on the actual timing or on the fractional time thereafter:

$$28, 29, 00 = .0$$
$$01, 02, 03 = .1$$
$$04, 05, 06 = .2$$
$$07, 08, 09 = .3$$
$$10, 11, 12 = .4$$
$$13, 14, 15 = .5$$
$$16, 17, 18 = .6$$
$$19, 20, 21 = .7$$
$$22, 23, 24 = .8$$
$$25, 26, 27 = .9$$

This two-frame error keeps the timings on the plus side of the equation, so the composer will never precede a cut or action.

SPOTTING NOTES

The first working material to be received by the composer from the music editor will be the spotting notes. The spotting notes and the designation for the individual cues are by reel number (1) with a letter M (for music) and a following number referring to the cue's placement in the reel (1). Thus, 1M1 indicates that this cue is in reel 1 and is the first cue in the reel.

The spotting notes would read as follows (see Figure 8.1):

1M1
01:00:20:00
030+0
2:00

Main title music starts as picture fades in on a long shot of bus driving along a country road. This scene covers many cuts of the little boy int. of bus. Music tails as the bus arrives at the orphanage. Note: It was suggested in the spotting session that the boy's theme should have an English horn lead.

1M2
01:04:22:15
393+12
:46

Music starts on girl staring down at little boy in hallway. The music will cover the scene of the little boy reacting to the girl, and the boy being led away by a teacher.
Music tails on cut to interior of dormitory.

Note: Girl's theme to have a flute lead.

Production: **DEAD POETS SOCIETY**
MUSIC SPOTTING NOTES

REEL 1
1M1   50.87   "BAG PIPES"
  s1:01:19:24   BAG PIPE MUSIC STARTS AS THEY RAISE SCHOOL BANNERS AND
  s1:02:10:20   START INTO CHURCH ASSEMBLY....MUSIC OUT AS THEY STOP PLAYING

REEL 2
2M1   58.33   "KEATING WHISTLES"
  s2:00:25:26   KIDS ARE SEATED IN CLASSROOM WHEN THE DOOR OPENS AND KEATING
  s2:01:24:06   COMES OUT WHISTLING......THIS CONTINUES UNTIL THE BOYS SURROUND
                       HIM IN ANTE ROOM OF HALLWAY.

2M2   3:42.50   "TO DANBURY"
  s2:04:07:08   KNOX IN HIS ROOM WRITES "SIEZE THE DAY", RIPS IT UP AND REACHES
  s2:07:49:23   FOR CHEMISTRY BOOK, MUSIC STARTS AS BOOK HITS THE
                       DESK.....THIS PLAYS THROUGH KNOX BEING DRIVEN TO THE DANBURY
                       HOUSE BY THE HEADMASTER AND TAILS AS GIRL SAYS"HELLO"

2M3   1:30.20   "STUDY GUITAR"
  s2:08:32:16   A GUITAR CAN BE HEARD IN THE STUDY HALL PLAYING SOFT
  s2:10:02:22   CHORDS...KNOX ENTERS AND TELLS EVERYONE HE'S IN LOVE...DOCTOR
                       HAGER ENTERS AND TELLS THEM "FIVE MINUTES", AND GUITAR STOPS
                       AFTER THIS LINE.

REEL 4
4M1   43.80   "WHO'S IN"
  s4:02:30:20   THE BOYS ARE TALKING ABOUT THE DEAD POETS SOCIETY ....MUSIC
  s4:03:14:14   STARTS AS NEAL TURNS ABRUPTLY BACK TO GROUP AND
                       ASKS.."WHO'S IN?....MUSIC PLAYS THROUGH THEIR GOING INTO
                       BUILDING AND TAILS ON CUT TO MAP.

Figure 8.1 Music spotting notes for *Dead Poets Society*.

On the left for the second note, 1M2 is the cue designation, and under that is the video time code 01:04:22:15, indicating the video frame on which the music is to start. Below that is the film footage of the start: 393 + 12. (If this is a film project, the telecine machine operator can include this footage on the videotape.) Then, below that is the overall timing or length of the cue: 46.

BREAKDOWN NOTES

Breakdown notes are minutely specific timings that pinpoint picture cuts, specific actions, start of dialogue and what is being said, end of dialogue, and all nuances within a scene. That is where the breakdown notes differ from the spotting notes. As noted earlier, the spotting notes only help a composer plan for composition and scoring, but she needs the breakdown notes from the music editor in order to actually begin writing music (see Figure 8.2).

An example of breakdown timing notes is as follows:

Video start	Film start	(Time and footage from the
00:40:21:18	251 + 12	projection start of reel)
Video Time	*Cue Time*	
00:40:21:18	:00.0	Music starts on cut to a night scene of semideserted downtown street, camera pans across street.
00:40:27:27	:06.3	Policeman comes into view by storefront.
00:40:30:18	:09.0	Man appears running out of store.
00:40:32:06	:10.6	Policeman yells, "Halt" as he starts to draw his gun.
00:40:32:18	:11.0	End line as he starts to aim gun.
00:40:33:00	:11.4 cut	Close-up policeman's face.
00:40:34:19	:12.7 cut	Full shot as gun fires.
00:40:35:00	:13.4	Policeman starts to run after man (and additional timings to the end of the scene).

Given this information, the *composer* will first select a tempo appropriate to the mood of the scene. Referring to charts that

Production: <u>DEAD POETS SOCIETY</u> Cue: <u>DESK STAND(14M1)</u>

Begins at <u>s14:06:57:07</u> in Reel 14

ABS. SMPTE #(30):	REL. TIME:		
			HEADMASTER IN KEATING CLASSROOM SAYS: 'ONE MORE OUTBURST AND YOU'RE OUT OF THIS SCHOOL"..
s14:06:57:07	0.00		MUSIC STARTS AFTER THIS LINE OVER KEATING LOOKING TOWARD HEADMASTER
s14:06:58:13	1.20		HIS EYES LOOK TO THE SIDE
s14:06:59:13	2.20		HEADMASTER CONTS: "LEAVE MR. KEATING"
s14:07:00:08	3.03		E.L.
s14:07:00:27	3.67		HIS EYES TO THE SIDE
s14:07:01:11	4.13		LOOKS BACK AT HEADMASTER
s14:07:01:24	4.57	CUT	HEADMASTER LOOKING TOWARD KEATING
s14:07:02:12	5.17		HEADMASTER: "I SAID LEAVE MR. KEATING"
s14:07:02:23	5.53		STILL TURNING HE: "OH CAPTAIN, MY CAPTAIN"
s14:07:03:23	6.53		BOY LOOKS DOWN
s14:07:04:14	7.23		E.L., HE STARES TOWARD KEATING
s14:07:05:05	7.93	CUT	CLOSE KEATING, LOOKING TOWARD HEADMASTER
s14:07:07:08	10.03		HE SMILES
s14:07:08:01	10.80		LOOKS TO THE SIDE
s14:07:08:26	11.63		LOWERS HEAD
s14:07:09:09	12.07		TURNS TO WALK AWAY
s14:07:10:14	13.23	CUT	HEADMASTER LOOKING TOWARD O.S. KEATING
s14:07:11:21	14.47		KEATING INTO FRAME PASSING CAM
s14:07:12:08	15.03		HE'S OUT OF FRAME, HEADMASTER CONTS TO STARE AFTER HIM

Page 1   4/23/89 4:54 PM

Figure 8.2a Breakdown notes for *Dead Poets Society* using SMPTE timing code.

Production: <u>PARENTHOOD</u>   Cue: <u>GARY'S REJECTION(6M1 REV)</u>

Begins <u>68/2</u> From Start of Reel 6

ABS. FEET/FRM(35):	REL. TIME:		
			GARY IS ON THE PHONE WITH HIS FATHER. HE ASKS IF HE CAN LIVE WITH HIM "...A FEW MONTHS." WE CUT TO HELEN WATCHING HIM, CUT CLOSE GARY'S FACE...
68/2	0.00		MUSIC STARTS A BEAT AFTER THIS CUT TO GARY ON THE PHONE
70/4	1.43		HE BLINKS
70/15	1.90		HE SOBS QUIETLY
74/6	4.20		HE: "OK"
75/13	5.13		HE BLINKS
77/0	5.93		SHIFTS HIS EYES
78/7	6.90		CLOSES EYES
78/12	7.10		QUIETLY SOBS AGAIN
79/6	7.50		STILL SOBBING HE PULLS PHONE AWAY TO HANG UP
80/3	8.07		PHONE OUT OF FRAME HE MOVES HEAD
80/14	8.50		O.S. PHONE ON HOOK
81/4	8.77		HE BLINKS
81/12	9.10		HIS HAND IN FRAME AS HE TURNS HIS HEAD
82/5	9.47	CUT	CLOSE HELEN WATCHING
83/2	10.00		AS SHE CLOSES HER EYES SHE CLICKS HER TONGUE
83/14	10.50		AS SHE OPENS HER EYES SHE INHALES DEEPLY AND TURNS HEAD TO THE SIDE
84/6	10.83		SHE SEPARATES HER HANDS
84/9	10.97		ONE HAND OUT OF FRAME
85/2	11.33		AS SHE STARTS TO PUT HAND TO HEAD SHE: "OH ANDY.."
86/5	12.13		SHE TOUCHES HER FOREHEAD

Page 1   7/9/89 11:50 AM

Figure 8.2b   Breakdown notes for *Parenthood* using feet per frame.

Production: <u>DEAD POETS SOCIETY</u> Cue: <u>DESK STAND(14M1)</u>   *4 FREE*

Begins at <u>s14:06:57:07</u> in Reel 14   *22-7*

TAC 17   1ˢᵗ BAR

ABS. SMPTE #(30):	REL. TIME:		
			HEADMASTER IN KEATING CLASSROOM SAYS: 'ONE MORE OUTBURST AND YOU'RE OUT OF THIS SCHOOL"..
s14:06:57:07	0.00		MUSIC STARTS AFTER THIS LINE OVER KEATING LOOKING TOWARD HEADMASTER
s14:06:58:13	1.20		HIS EYES LOOK TO THE SIDE
s14:06:59:13	2.20		HEADMASTER CONTS: "LEAVE MR. KEATING"
s14:07:00:08	3.03		E.L.
s14:07:00:27	3.67		HIS EYES TO THE SIDE
s14:07:01:11	4.13		LOOKS BACK AT HEADMASTER
s14:07:01:24	4.57	CUT	HEADMASTER LOOKING TOWARD KEATING
s14:07:02:12	5.17		HEADMASTER: "I SAID LEAVE MR. KEATING"
s14:07:02:23	5.53		STILL TURNING HE: "OH CAPTAIN, MY CAPTAIN"
s14:07:03:23	6.53		BOY LOOKS DOWN
s14:07:04:14	7.23		E.L., HE STARES TOWARD KEATING
s14:07:05:05	7.93	CUT	CLOSE KEATING, LOOKING TOWARD HEADMASTER
s14:07:07:08	10.03		HE SMILES
s14:07:08:01	10.80		LOOKS TO THE SIDE
s14:07:08:26	11.63		LOWERS HEAD
s14:07:09:09	12.07		TURNS TO WALK AWAY
s14:07:10:14	13.23	CUT	HEADMASTER LOOKING TOWARD O.S. KEATING
s14:07:11:21	14.47		KEATING INTO FRAME PASSING CAM
s14:07:12:08	15.03		HE'S OUT OF FRAME, HEADMASTER CONTS TO STARE AFTER HIM
s14:07:12:22	15.50	CUT	CLOSE NEAL LLOKING DOWN
s14:07:14:04	16.90		TURNS HEAD TO SIDE

CLICK 24
21-7

Page 1   4/27/89 9:38 AM

Figure 8.2c Breakdown notes for *Dead Poets Society* that have been marked and "adjusted."

translate timing into beat numbers for a given tempo (these charts constitute the Knudsen book, to be discussed), the composer can determine on what beat number the man runs out of the store, the dialogue begins and ends, the gunshot occurs, and the chase starts. If, in this tempo, the beats correspond to moments in the picture (for example, a strong down beat landing firmly on the cut to the policeman's face), then the composer can begin writing music. Otherwise, she will need to try a slightly faster or slower tempo until she achieves compatibility.

The music to cover this scene might start with a blues feeling up to :09.0 where the man runs out of the store, then build tension to the gunshot at :12.7 (making certain that the music does not step on the line "Halt"), then immediately change into chase music on the timing of :13.4, and change again for the death scene at the end. Without the specific timings in the breakdown notes, a composer would not be able to accent specific cuts or actions within the scene.

The music editor must calculate precisely the breakdown timings, which could require a great deal of math. For example, to arrive at the figure of :06.3 where the policeman comes into view, the SMPTE time code number appearing on that frame must be subtracted from the time code of the start of the cue:

$$
\begin{array}{r}
00:40:27:27 \\
-00:40:21:18 \\
\hline
00:00:06:09
\end{array}
$$

This gives the hours (00), minutes (00), seconds (06), and frames (09). The composer needs a timing in seconds and tenths of seconds, so the count of :09 frames must be further converted to tenths of seconds. Then, :09 frames divided by 3 converts to 0.3 a second. Therefore, SMPTE time 00:00:06:09 = :06.3 seconds real time. If the division is not even and there are one or two frames left over, then move to the next tenth of a second. The human eye momentarily retains the image of the previous cut to validate the musical delay of a frame or two even when the timing is exact.

Fortunately, all the information for correct conversions, including drop or nondrop frame, 59.94 or 60 Hertz, can be preprogrammed into a computer that converts all of the SMPTE time code numbers into relative true time.

The preparation for the scoring stage must be meticulous, because any error is costly. Specifically, the amount of time used to correct errors on the stage is figured by multiplying the number of musicians at $1.00 per minute and the stage time at $6.00 per minute. If there are 60 musicians in a scoring session, a ten-minute correction equals $600.00 for musicians plus $60.00 in stage time. And there is no way to estimate the cost of the time lost from the life span of a music editor because of the anxiety endured while making the correction.

THE KNUDSEN BOOK

The Knudsen book has been for many years and remains the bible for film composers. It contains computerized readouts in tabular form that enable a composer to specify a tempo for a given timing and confirm that a specific beat within the cue will correspond to a particular moment in the picture. The book's calculations are based on the standard 24-frames-per-second film speed. Thus, the book is the standard device by which film composers determine tempo.

When you put a small punch or scratch in the sound area of a solid piece of film every 24 frames and run this film on an optical machine, you will hear a noise, called a click, every second. This is one of an infinite number of possible tempos. During a musical performance (live or recorded), the tempo is maintained by a conductor or is backed by a metronome, click track (punched film run on an optical machine), or computer-programmed electronics.

For film composing, Carol Knudsen took a 35 mm film frame, which has four perforations, and divided that again by two, splitting each frame into eighths. Tempos are thus set in the number of frames and eighths of a frame between clicks or beats. A 24-0 click tempo, for example, indicates a click every 24 frames and 0 eighths of a frame, or 60 per minute. To illustrate the use of the Knudsen book, assume a composer wanted the down beat of the second bar of a cue to correspond to a cut in the picture. The composer sees in the breakdown notes that the cut occurs :04.5 seconds from the beginning of the cue. Assuming 4/4 time, so that the down beat of the second bar is the fifth beat, the composer can learn from the Knudsen book that a 27-0 click tempo would match perfectly that beat to the cut.

This resource has eliminated a great deal of multiplication and division. The long way of calculating the same information is to multiply the number of seconds by the number of frames per second. In this case, 4.5 (seconds) × 24 (frames) = 108 frames. Dividing 108 (frames) by 4 (number of beats) gives 27 frames. To be on the cut on the fifth beat, you have to record to a 27-0 frame click. Because of the time-consuming math involved, there are few working composers who have not obtained a Knudsen book.

Another excellent book on this topic was written by Ruby Raksin and is called *Technical Handbook of Mathematics for Motion Picture Music Synchronization.*

As the composer writes a cue, she will indicate at the top of each sketch the tempo in film frames and eighths of a frame between each beat, and the number of warning or preparatory beats, called *free beats,* that should be built into the click track or metronome program for the scoring stage.

PREPARING FOR THE SCORING STAGE

A major part of the music editor's function is to help the composer prepare for the scoring session. Using the breakdown notes, the composer can write the score for the production. Part of this task, as discussed above, is to determine the correct tempo for each cue and carefully note important points where music and picture must match. The composer and music editor must make sure that the conductor of the scoring session (who may or may not be the composer) will have, if required, visual and aural references available during the session, ensuring that tempos are followed and important moments in the picture are punctuated.

A conductor in a scoring session will use one or several references to make sure she is conducting in the correct tempo and that the cue will match the picture. There may be an aural reference, such as a regular beat setting the tempo. This beat may be produced by an optical click track, a metronome (mechanical, digital, or computerized), or a preprogrammed sound track that is usually part of a videotape. Visual references will be integrated into the picture shown during the scoring session and are generally either *streamers* (long, diagonal lines across the screen) or *punch clusters* (prominent blank spots in the picture) (see Figure 8.3).

OPTICAL CLICK TRACKS

Despite the standard use of the digital metronome and the growing use of related computerized devices, optical click tracks are still used occasionally in film productions when a scene requires a complex change of tempo within a cue. When building an optical click track, the music editor uses a length of solid-backed 35 mm film (yellow leader) and a punch that perforates three small, narrow perforations in the sound track area of the film.

Each punch, a specified number of frames and perforations apart, reflects the tempo dictated by the musical score. This is called an *optical click track*. When this track is placed on an optical sound machine, the solid area of the yellow leader is silent until a punched perforation passes by the optical light, making a clicking sound.

On the scoring stage, the picture and optical click track are interlocked to run simultaneously. The optical click track, running in sync with the picture, starts and stops clicking at predetermined times in concert with the score.

Because an optical sound machine is not always available on scoring stages, it is sometimes necessary to have the optical click track transferred to 35 mm magnetic tape at another facility and then taken to the scoring stage.

Clicks are of great help to musicians, as it is easier for the players to maintain tempo by listening to the clicks while reading their instrumental parts than it is for them to have to watch the conductor and read at the same time.

Many times a conductor will use clicks only to establish the tempo. In these instances, the music editor will start the digital metronome for the introductory or free clicks, and then turn them off on the down beat of the first bar. The introductory clicks establish the tempo ensuring a uniform attack on the opening note. Then the conductor, watching the seconds clock, can maintain, increase, or decrease the tempo of the music as he desires.

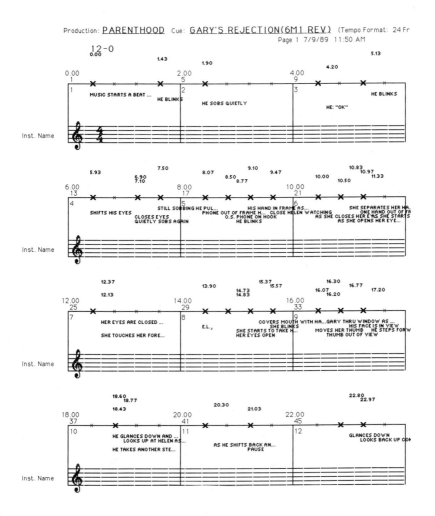

Figure 8.3 Bar breakdown for *Parenthood.*

STREAMERS AND PUNCH CLUSTERS

Streamers are long diagonal lines placed on the picture part of a film or videotape to indicate the start of introductory (free) clicks, the start of the music, changes of tempo, picture cuts or specific actions, and the end of the cue. Punch clusters are holes punched in the picture of film or blank circles of picture programmed into videotape, also for the purpose of maintaining and indicating changes in tempo. Punch clusters are usually placed every other frame, for a total sequence of six frames. These markings on a film or videotape provide a reference for the conductor during the scoring session, indicating the down beat of bars.

To make a streamer on film, a music editor uses a device called a *streamer board,* which simply holds the film in place and provides a guide so the music editor can remove emulsion from the film in the desired shape. There has never been a standard in the industry for a board or other machine by which streamers may be applied. However, some of the major studios still have elaborate mechanical devices for putting a streamer on a piece of film, although with these Rube Goldberg devices you run the risk of tearing up your film.

The basic streamer board is a three-foot-long flat piece of wood or metal, with a center slot running its length and wide enough to accommodate a piece of 35 mm film. The section of the film to be streamered is placed in the streamer board, emulsion side up. A hinged flap of the board folds over the film. This flap is angled and acts as a guide for the music editor, who, using a stylus, scrapes the emulsion from the film to create a clear three-foot diagonal line about one-eighth inch wide. A hole will be punched in the last frame of the streamer to accentuate its ending. The top of the streamer starts on the left side of the picture frame, and as it descends it moves across the screen diagonally until it disappears in a white flash created by a single punch. Some of the streamers will be stained with different colored brush pens. A warning streamer, to indicate the start of the introductory (warning or free) clicks, is colored yellow; a green streamer signifies the start of music; a blue streamer indicates the clicks will stop; and a red streamer indicates the end of the cue. This color scheme may be modified by the composer or music editor to suit her individual taste. The standard length of a streamer is three feet (two-second duration), but the length of the streamer is merely an idiosyncrasy of the individual composer. Some composers prefer four-foot streamers, and there is at least one who relies on a five-foot length.

Although these basic manual methods are still used by many music editors, particularly on low-budget films, technology is rapidly making them obsolete.

As an example of the creation of streamers and punch clusters, consider a cue given to the music editor from the composer with the provision for a 27-0 click track and four free beats, and assuming 4/4 time. The music editor will prepare that cue for the scoring stage by scribing a green streamer to the frame where the music will start, and a yellow streamer four beats back, using the 27-0 tempo as a reference to determine precisely how many frames four beats represents ($4 \times 27 = 108$).

MUSIC EDITING SYSTEMS FOR VIDEOTAPE

As previously noted, the music editor receives a complete videotape of the production regardless of whether the final medium is film or video. More and more film productions are using video for all of their music postproduction tasks because of the tremendous flexibility and power offered by modern electronics. Thus, most music editors and composers possess technical abilities in both film and video.

Most music editors currently use one or more of three computerized systems designed for video: the Cue System, the Spellbinder-Streamline, and the Auricle. Each system offers both similar and unique capabilities; most music editors prefer the one system that most closely fills his or her needs.

The Cue System is popular because it enables the music editor easily to create and change spotting notes, breakdown notes, and bar charts. An editor can program a cue into the system and then print out the bar charts to reflect small changes, a task that requires hours when using paper and pencil. An editor can make small changes in the timing of a cue, and the system will automatically and quickly make appropriate adjustments to other parts of the score. The Cue System also acts as a very precise Knudsen book, finding tempos that will enable selected beats to correspond to events in the picture, such as a cut.

The Spellbinder-Streamline system places tempo beats, streamers, and punches on videotape with flexibility and precision that is not possible with standard film techniques. For example, the precision of the film-based Knudsen book in establishing tempos is limited by the size of its smallest unity of measurement, eighths of a frame (about 0.005 seconds). Digital-based tempo machines such as the Spellbinder-Streamline can use a much smaller unit of measurement—for example, SMPTE time code—thereby offering more numerous and precise options. In addition, these systems allow an editor easily to change tempos or make other special alterations within a cue. The ability of a system to accommodate an *accelerando* (increased tempo) or a *ritardando* (decreased tempo) can save a music editor hours of time. Accented down beats can be programmed, streamers in a variety of colors can be applied on the videotape, and punches of various sizes and duration are available. Because the system is electronically based, punches and streamers are not permanent as they would be in a piece of film.

The Auricle was developed as a more sophisticated metronomic counter for composers. The Auricle is preprogrammed by the composer and brought to the scoring stage, where the music editor triggers the machine, operating it as she might a digital metronome. Its developers are making constant upgrades to further the capabilities of this system to include the streamers and clicks that are incorporated into the Streamline System, as well as automated starts. Working with the Auricle in its present condition, on a scoring session, one can silence clicks for any given area, turn the clicks on for optional areas that the composer is having difficulty conducting, and be flexible enough to change tempo or meter with speed and accuracy. This is a system that is easily handled by composers when writing a score, and there are composers who would not work without it. Its value to the music editor, with the exception of the scoring stage, is limited at this time.

THE NEWMAN SYSTEM

Streamers and punches are also used within a cue to assist the composer when conducting in *free time*. Free time designates a cue that is not recorded to regular clicks or a click track. The advantage of conducting to free time lies in the ability of the conductor to have a cue flow freely, without a consistent metronomic beat which sometimes has a tendency to make a cue feel regimented. Thus, although free time does not use a click track, the conductor will need streamers and punches just to make sure the cue is generally maintaining the correct time and to ensure that the key moments in the picture are correctly punctuated. For example, if, on a free timing sketch, the composer has indicated a timing of :32 seconds to the down beat of the eleventh bar (beat 41), when the meter is 4/4 time, the music editor would calculate:

1. :32 seconds times 24 (the number of film frames in a second) equals 768 frames.
2. 768 (number of frames in :32) divided by 40 (number of beats in 10 full bars—down beat of the eleventh bar, beat 41, completes the 40th beat and has no time value) equals 19.2 frames between beats.
3. The click track needed is a 19.2 to hit the down beat of the eleventh bar or 41st beat at :32.
4. Four beats times 19.2 frames equals 76.8 frames per bar of music.
5. 76.8 divided by 24 (number of frames in a second) equals 3.2 seconds per bar.

To prepare this film for free time recording on the scoring stage, a streamer will be placed to the start of the cue (:00). Then punches are placed for the downbeat of the second bar (:03.2), then again for the down beat of the third bar (:06.4), skipping the fourth and going to the down beat of the fifth (:12.8), a set of punches for the down beat of the seventh bar (:19.2), again for the ninth bar (25,6), followed by a streamer indicating the end of the cue (:32). The conductor will follow the first streamer for the down beat of the music, and when the punches come into frame (:03.2) it flashes out from the screen and immediately tells the composer if the conducting is too fast or too slow. By the time the second set of punches flashes (:06.4), the conducting should have stabilized to the extent that only every other bar is necessary to indicate a down beat. Streamers are used within the cue to indicate picture cuts or definitive action, changes of tempo, grand pauses, *fermatas* (a discretionary prolongation of a note or rest by the conductor or performer), or any other effect the composer feels would require the exactitude of a streamer.

This mode of preparation, called the *Newman system*, afforded the best insurance for a composer to be at the right place at the right time musically. It was devised by the late Alfred Newman, a formidable composer who, for many years, was head of the music department for 20th Century Fox Studios. If a composer wishes to score using the Newman system with videotape, the Streamline System computer will program and produce all of the streamers and punches required.

· 9 ·

The Scoring Stage

CHARACTERISTICS OF A SCORING STAGE

Almost every scoring stage has a huge, thick door, which some-times has the type of handle found on meat market cold storage locker doors. On a scoring stage, this door is, of course, for sound isolation. However, it is incongruous that the interior of such an artistic environment can be entered only by a display of brute strength in pulling open that behemoth of a portal. There are, of course, smaller stages with double, not so thick doors, which con-trive to imprison the sound by capturing it within a three-foot confined air space. Either approach is an obstacle course for anyone carrying an instrument, toting scores, or weighing less than 175 pounds.

Once someone has aided you in your access, you will find yourself in a very large windowless room with an extraordinarily high ceiling, a large silver screen on the back wall, floor-to-ceiling adjustable baffles on the walls, innumerable music stands with their accompanying chairs, and microphones positioned every-where (see Figure 9.1). The baffles are waffle-shaped panels that

Figure 9.1 An example of a classic scoring stage. Note the high ceiling and the baffles.

deflect or absorb sound, control or isolates individual instruments, eliminating echoes and other sound disturbances. This allows better quality sound recording. The picture being scored can be displayed on the screen where the conductor can see it. The stage will also be outfitted with a digital metronome for tempo reference purposes (see Figure 9.2) and a seconds clock so the conductor on the podium can monitor the length of the music (see Figure 9.3).

MICROPHONE SETUP

In recording a large orchestra, one microphone is used for the concert (first chair) violin, and perhaps six or eight more to cover the remaining string sections: violins, violas, cellos, and string bass. The harp has an individual microphone, and so do each of the woodwind sections: flute, clarinet, bassoon, English horn, oboe, and saxophone. Each brass section, trumpets, trombones, French horns, and tuba, will have its own microphone. Each instrument in rhythm and percussion sections: piano, electronic keyboards, harp-

Figure 9.2a The music editor's desk. Notice the digital metronome, microphone, and control buttons for seconds clock.

Figure 9.2b A closeup of the digital metronome set for very slow tempo, 30 frames per second.

Figure 9.3 The conductor's podium and time clock. The equipment is deceptively simple for the precision of the work.

sichord, timpani, bass drum, bongos, cymbals, bells, chimes, and other percussive devices will be recorded with a microphone.

THE RECORDING BOOTH

Behind the podium, isolated by dual air-spaced panes of cantilevered glass, is the control booth. The interior of this booth is impressive, featuring an elongated audio control panel with innumerable controls to heighten or lessen, round out or thin down, the volume and quality of the particular sound of any instrument being played. Large overhead speakers, recording machines, video machines, and cables everywhere allow those within the booth to monitor and record the scoring session and project the appropriate picture on the scoring stage's screen (see Figure 9.4a and 9.4b).

Figure 9.4a A typical recording booth is actually much larger and more complex than the term "booth" implies.

Figure 9.4b The control panel and assorted patch cables.

THE MUSIC ENGINEER

The individual who sits behind this board and controls the volume and color of the sound being recorded is referred to as the music engineer. The primary prerequisites for this position are musicianship and a very good set of ears, although technical expertise is also required. The orchestral sound balance will vary slightly with every music engineer when recording an orchestra. Each engineer has his or her own conception of the best sound and how to record it.

THE RECORDIST

The music engineer controls the destiny of the musical instruments, whereas the recordist is responsible for making sure the sound from the scoring stage is accurately taped. The recordist logs which instruments are recorded on which tracks. This is an exacting function and must be maintained with the utmost precision. When a cue is recorded, if a bad note is heard or an instrument enters at the wrong time, rather than rerecording the entire cue the recordist can access just the track or tracks containing the error. The recordist can rerecord only the instrument responsible for the error or can simply erase the problem section. The recordist is sometimes responsible for operating the video machines and setting up each cue in its proper start.

In the case of vocals or solo instruments, several renditions may be recorded to the music track, thereby producing several similar but not identical tracks. The recordist can *checkerboard* the recording, punching (switching) back and forth between tracks to get the best phrasing (style)—track 1 for the start, trace 3 for the second phrase, back to track 1 for the third, track 2 for the fourth, and so on. Recordists must have a good sense of timing and be adroit and familiar with the numerous sophisticated machines they must operate.

The most commonly used recorder for film scoring is fast changing from the 24-track analog recorder to the Mitsubishi one-inch 32-track or the half-inch 48-track Sony, both of which are digital recorders.

TRACK ASSIGNMENTS

Each of the microphones on the scoring stage leads through the mixing panel to a two-inch 24-track magnetic analog, a one-inch 48-track digital (Sony), or a half-inch 32-track digital (Mitsubishi) recording machine.

Because there are only 24, 32, or 48 tracks available for recording, and two of those are used for the SMPTE time code and the 60-cycle Hertz sync pulse, each microphone cannot have an individual track, as a full orchestra generally requires more than 48 tracks. Therefore, the music engineer will have to combine orchestra sounds as he makes the track assignments.

Typically, in the string section, the concertmaster will be assigned to track 1. The high strings will be combined on track 2, the midrange violas will take track 3, the cellos can be on track 4, and the string bass will take track 5.

The percussionist will be playing timpani, bells, chimes, cymbal, and bass drum, each with its own microphone. However, because the percussionist will play only one instrument at a time, the microphones for those instruments can all be assigned to track 6. The oboe and the English horn are very similar and generally play at separate times within the piece, so they can both go on track 7.

This procedure continues until all the instruments are accommodated. The music engineer will vary the track assignments on different cues to keep the lead instruments isolated and make modifications when the number of orchestra players decreases. The last two tracks of all tape recorders are always assigned the sync pulse and the SMPTE time code.

THE CONDUCTOR

At one time, all the major studios had an on-staff conductor. The studio would contract with a composer to write a score, and on the scoring date the composer would stay in the mixing booth. This allowed the composer to supervise the music engineer, ensuring that the music was being recorded exactly as the composer wished.

Now, independent production companies and the major studios contractually call for a composer to compose, orchestrate, and conduct the score. Unfortunately, the talent for composing wonderful music does not automatically make a good conductor. Some composers are excellent conductors and would not delegate that responsibility; some even say conducting is the only fun they have on a project. Others who are less gifted as conductors are well advised to hire a conductor for the benefit of the musicians and also as a matter of economy, as they themselves are difficult to follow. Some composers conduct metrically, giving the standard motion for the beats, whereas others conduct to the feeling of the music, and that is not always easy for the players to follow. Few composers will admit to inadequacies regarding their abilities on the podium, so the musicians are eternally grateful to those who do recognize their limitations and bring a conductor to the session.

In some situations, the music contractor or music editor will conduct rehearsals while the composer is in the booth acquainting the music engineer with the mix he prefers. The composer will take the podium for the actual recording. This allows the composer to familiarize the music engineer with the subtleties of the score.

Composers find that in addition to being musicians, they often have to be magicians. There is a constant search for new and innovative sounds to give the underscore a unique and fresh approach. This pursuit of new sounds produces a continual influx of new faces and instruments on the scoring stages, and makes unusual demands on the orchestra players. For example, a keyboard player might be asked to hold the sustain pedal down on the acoustic piano while the percussionist empties a bucket of golf balls on the lower strings to acquire a marvelously effective "death chord." This need for innovation brings some very strange instruments to the scoring stage. For example, how many readers have heard the sound of a "water bucket," or would recognize an "Indian bull roar"?

THE MUSICIANS

There was a time when all the major studios had their own orchestras on a permanent weekly payroll. Members of these orchestras were appropriately called studio musicians, and were under exclusive contract to one or another major studio. Nothing comparable exists today. *Studio musician* now denotes a musician who takes a scoring call regardless of the studio. In Hollywood, for example, you will find some of the musicians who record at the one-time MGM (later Lorimar, then Warner's, now Columbia) sound stage on Monday recording at the Warner Bros. Studio on Tuesday, while on Wednesday they are playing at Paramount Studios. They'll be at 20th Century Fox on Thursday and at Studio Center on Friday. During the busy season, several hundred musicians are necessary to meet television and feature production requirements in Hollywood alone.

These musicians, who are in constant demand, are comparable to the very best musicians found anywhere in the world. Their abilities in sight reading, instrumental doubling, and jazz and classical performance, combined with their reliability, flexibility, versatility, adaptability, and creativity, keep them constantly busy. With every piece of original underscore presented to these musicians, it is the first time they have seen those notes. In scoring for episodic television programs, the cue is played once to familiarize the players with the music and to check notes, then a second time for dynamics. On the third playing, it will be recorded.

When ethnic material is part of the score, musicians are called who can produce that authentic sound, whether it be Dixieland, Far Eastern, Caribbean, *mariachi,* or an Irish penny whistle. Whatever the need, musicians who can get that special sound will be located and called by the contractor for the session.

With a picture where stately grandeur or epochal scenes are to be underscored, large orchestras of 80 or more musicians are assembled. The number of musicians for the average feature is closer to 65. Scoring orchestras for episodic television with lower music budgets will average in the neighborhood of 27 players. The fewer players there are, the greater the challenge to composers to orchestrate as full and rich a sound as possible. These average numbers are based on traditional acoustic instrumental underscoring. The integration of electronic keyboards, which can emulate entire string sections as well as other instruments, can drastically reduce the size of an orchestra or even eradicate it altogether.

Let us assume that for our hypothetical scoring session, there are 65 musicians. The music engineer will have the orchestral sections and the recording microphones arranged on the scoring stage in the proper position to capture the best acoustic sound.

RECORDING

Scoring sessions very greatly in size, complexity, and duration. Simple, electronically created scores for short productions, such as a commercial, may take only a few hours and require a minimal crew. Big-budget motion picture scores may take many weeks. Obviously, since time is money—a lot of money—the goal is to achieve recordings that please the key people in as little time as possible.

On the first day of our hypothetical scoring session, the music librarian, who is responsible for maintaining and distributing the written music, places the instrumental parts, written out by the copyists, on the appropriate music stands. The copyist remains on the scoring stage to make any corrections or changes requested by the composer.

When the first cue is rehearsed, with the aid of the Urie digital metronome and the seconds clock, both the conductor and the music editor know immediately if the timing is correct. Sometimes there is no need for a projected picture or videotape. Even when scoring with available projection facilities, there are many instances when cues will be recorded wild (without picture) using the digital metronome and seconds clock to ensure the proper timing.

The orchestra members face the conductor's podium in the front of the room. The music editor's table is usually to the right and slightly behind the podium. Mounted in front of the podium, facing the conductor, is a schoolroom-type clock with a large sweep hand calibrated in seconds. On this podium the composer is in full view of the orchestra and in a position to watch both the screen and the seconds clock while conducting.

Facing the orchestra from the podium, the grouping on the left is the string section. The center section comprises the woodwinds, and on the right side there is the brass section. In the far center you will find the percussionists with their variety of paraphernalia, including keyboards, timpani, chimes, treebells, and the like. If there is a sit-down drummer, he will also be in the back of the room in an isolation booth.

Before the orchestra settles down to the business at hand, the conductor requests an A note from the pianist. After the pianist strikes the note, each musician tunes her instrument to that A. The piano, which has been carefully tuned prior to the scoring, thus serves as a reference for the entire orchestra.

The engineer might request individuals or sections to play a part of the score or just build a triad (a harmonious blend of three musical parts) so that a proper level and blend can be obtained on the mixing panel. When the engineer feels the settings are correct, the conductor will rehearse the cue. This is the time for the conductor and musicians to check for any miscopied notes and make any minor adjustments in the score.

The cue will be rehearsed as often as necessary by the conductor until all the nuances and shadings necessary for the finest rendition of the music cue are achieved. The orchestrator (arranger) may be in the recording booth, following the score, to alert the mixer for the entrances of the various instruments.

When scoring a feature, there are usually two other individuals listening in the booth, the producer and the director. At these rehearsals, they do not offer much of a critique, as this is a technical exercise on the part of the conductor and the music engineer to perfect the performance and the recording of the orchestra. Nevertheless, everyone is cognizant of their presence.

When the rehearsal is complete, the engineer is ready to record, and the film or video is on its proper starting point, the engineer starts the recording machine and announces, "Rolling." The picture will appear either on the big screen or on a television monitor (sometimes both). The music editor makes the announcement, "1M1 take 1," punches the preset digital metronome to activate the free clicks on the disappearance of the yellow streamer, and starts the seconds clock on the down beat as the green streamer ends. The orchestra plays the cue, and when the conductor hits a *fermata* (a long, sustained note) on the last note, the music editor turns off the digital clicks. The editor stops the clock when the *fermata* has died away.

The music editor keeps a log that notes the cue number, take number, and timing, and describes the mood and pace of each cue. The cue and take designations are similar to the records kept in picture productions. Each cue may need to be played and recorded several times before an acceptable recording is achieved. Each attempt represents a sequentially numbered take. The cue number in the scoring session matches that established in the spotting and breakdown notes. The foregoing example, "1M1 take 1," represents the first take of cue 1M1. Upon completion of the first take, the conductor leaves the podium, enters the control booth, and listens to a playback against the picture. The musicians also can watch the screen or monitor and listen to the results of their performance. If all the technical and aesthetic aspects of the take are acceptable to everyone present, the cue is finished and the session can proceed with the next cue. If problems occur or changes are desired, part or all of the cue may need to be rerecorded in a subsequent take or takes.

Scoring to picture is a descendant of playing a piano to accompany silent pictures in the days of the nickelodeon. Such accompaniment was not a haphazard improvisation on the part of a piano player, but a specific, well-thought-out piece of music, written by a composer and furnished to the theater by the production company to complement the film. The projection of picture in a scoring session today is a holdover from those bygone days. *Scoring to picture* refers to music cues recorded to a projected picture. Once recorded, the cue can be played back against picture for review by the composer, director, and producer.

Only if a composer uses the Newman system, with the integrated streamers and punches on the picture, is picture projection while scoring obligatory. There are also occasions when a musician will be asked to duplicate the musical performance of an actor on the screen playing a musical instrument. In this case the musician will position herself to be able to watch the screen and play at the same time. This common occurrence takes place after the full orchestra has been dismissed.

It is less costly and less time consuming to score without projection. The question is, why bother if it's not necessary?

The answer is that producers and directors want the luxury of hearing the music while watching the picture in order to eliminate any surprises on the dubbing or sweetening stage. With the picture projected or viewed on a video monitor, they are assured that the music fits the scene, the music is emotionally correct, and the composer has captured the mood of the scene. Thus, although scoring with projection may not be strictly necessary, most productions include this feature.

On the scoring stage, the recording order of the music cues is dictated by the number of instruments needed for a particular cue. After recording of the main title, end title, a scenic cue, and any cues for which a full orchestral sound is required, the number of musicians decreases. The first section to be released might be the string section; the brass and percussion players are saved for the action and chase cues. The number of musicians continues to decrease with each session until the last day of recording, when there may be only a small group left for the source music or single instrumentation cues.

PRODUCERS AND DIRECTORS

The producer or director will have a great influence on the amount of time spent on a recording session. Both the producer and the director will express their opinion of the music after the first playback, when they have had an opportunity to hear the music against the scene as it was being recorded and also on the playback for the composer.

The producer and director are usually familiar with the musical theme or themes, as the composer will have played these for them on a piano and received their approval before going forward with the writing. However, there is a big difference between hearing a skeletal theme played on a piano and hearing it played with a full orchestral arrangement. Although the composer and the musicians may create the musical facet of the film or video, the director and the producer have overall responsibility for the production. The final score must ultimately match their vision of the work. In the majority of cases, the director and producer will be ecstatically appreciative of the music playing against the picture, and the scoring session will proceed successfully.

There are, however, sessions fraught with minor or even serious problems. Individual idiosyncrasies will be voiced, and there's no guessing what underlying personal tastes will influence the producer's or director's reaction. There might be a request to have the lead melody played on an oboe instead of a violin. There might be a feeling that the music is too heavy or too light, steps on the dialogue, or is too fast or too slow for the action in the scene. Some of these problems can be remedied immediately on the next playing simply by having the conductor rework the score. In the extreme case, the cue would be totally unacceptable, and the conductor would move on to the next cue, knowing that the first cue would have to be rewritten. Everyone involved, particularly the composer, hopes that things will run smoothly. However, if the director or producer requests musical changes, the session might go into overtime. When the production company has the fiscal responsibility for the scoring session, then it is their cost, as they are the ones who are picking up the overtime charges.

On the other hand, if the composer has agreed to a flat contractual sum to supply the entire music package—that is, paying for the stage time, the arranger, the copyist, the musicians, and other costs—then any consequent requests for musical changes by a producer or director results in time consumption and possible financial disaster for the composer.

When an episodic television segment is being scored, you will seldom find either the director or the producer present, as their work schedule calls for them to be dealing with upcoming episodes. An associate producer usually represents them on the scoring stage.

THE COMPOSER AS MUSICIAN

If, at a scoring session, a piano part is not written into the score but is needed for a background source cue, then rather than call a pianist to provide one piece of source music, the composer may play the piano for that cue. There are some composers who have gained their reputation through performing on a particular instrument, and they will be sure to integrate a playing part for themselves into the session. Some will leave the podium and let the clicks maintain meter while they take their place with the other musicians. One composer had a microphone placed by the podium to facilitate his conducting and playing the trumpet at the same time. If the orchestra is a small group, the composer can sit with the musicians and, with the help of a digital metronome to maintain tempo, perform on every cue.

A composer is completely responsible for every piece of music written for the picture. Composing is a lonely job, composers are not having a great deal of fun while they sit in their studio writing the score. The joy of writing music comes with hearing it played, and the further enhancement of that joy is to be included as one of the performing musicians. Although it is rare for a composer to join the orchestra as a player, and it is certainly not always possible or even recommended, it does occasionally take place, and it's always a pleasure for the composer.

ELECTRONIC INSTRUMENTS

There are some compositional groups and individual composers who score films with electronic sounds in a music studio in their home. This negates the need for a scoring session altogether. Some composers will emulate orchestral sounds, whereas others will concentrate on the new and unique sounds possible from the diverse electronic instruments.

Sampling is the recording and conversion to digital form of the natural sound of any acoustic instrument or sound effect, ultimately entered into the memory bank of a computer. The keyboard artist or programmer can alter the pitch of notes or effects within the full range of the musical scale by means of the computer's keyboard. By this means, beginning with an acoustic or electronic base, a full orchestration for any piece of music can be developed.

The element of time is the most important aspect of a one-person electronic score. In attempting to duplicate an orchestral sound, each section of the orchestra must be played individually and built in layers on a 24-, 32-, or 48-track tape recorder and then dubbed down for use on the final mix or sweetening stage. Thus, although only one person may be required to produce an electronic score, that person can take much longer to record the score than would an orchestra assembled on a scoring stage.

The versatility of synthesizers and other electronic instruments in emulating orchestral sounds is of great concern to musicians whose livelihood depends on playing their acoustic instrument. Calls for acoustic musicians are diminishing and the calls that do come in are for a shorter duration. A picture might use a full orchestra for the main title and end credits, but the remaining cues might be scored with electronic instruments.

Innovative electronic sounds can be integrated into orchestral arrangements or they may stand alone. The days of the acoustic purist are gone; we have a generation raised on electronic music that expects these sounds when they watch and listen to television programs or attend a screening in a theater.

Composers, when integrating electronic sounds with an acoustic score, find it expeditious to record the electronics first and then augment (sweeten) with an orchestral recording at a later date. It is not desirable to take the time needed to find the desired texture of electronic sound while an orchestra waits. Some composers will use electronics to emulate orchestral sounds, whereas others will concentrate on the new, unique sounds possible from the various electronic instruments.

METRONOMIC TEMPO MACHINES

On a scoring stage, all of the musicians, the conductor, and the music editor wear headsets. At a predetermined time, the music editor starts the digital metronome that broadcasts a consistently recurring clicking sound, preset by the music editor, to all of the headsets. The conductor and musicians will hear the clicking sound and use it as their guide as it sets and maintains the tempo.

For film and videotape productions, a digital metronome can be set to any frame and an eighth of a frame to produce a consistent clicking sound in the required tempo. The program of the digital metronome, included on every music scoring stage, is based on the consistent speed of all film; 35 mm, 16 mm, or 8 mm, running at 24 frames per second. There are four perforations on each frame of 35 mm film. The digital metronome divides a frame into eighths, and this division gives the digital metronome a greater variety of tempos than the classical metronome.

Although the settings on a digital metronome are based on 35 mm film frames, time in seconds and tenths of seconds is the real criteria for the calculations of the metronome (click) setting. Thus, the metronome can work for video as accurately as it does for film, because, although film runs at 24 frames per second and video at approximately 30 frames per second, music tempo for either can be expressed in clicks per second (or tenths of a second). The metronome can be used for any type of recording where a consistent meter needs to be established.

A setting for the digital metronome is composed of the number of film frames, in full frames and eighths of frames, between the clicks. For example, at a setting of 24-0, you will hear a click every 24 frames, or every second (since the standard film speed is 24 frames per second). In 4/4 time, in which there are four full beats per measure, one measure will be four seconds long.

A metronome setting of 18-0 will make the clicks faster, increasing the tempo. 18-0 will produce one click every 18 frames. In 4/4 time, four beats thus equals 72 frames; at 24 frames per second, a measure at the 18-0 setting is three seconds long. Similarly, a setting of 21-0 will produce measures in 4/4 time that are three and a half seconds in duration.

The vast majority of composers writing music for episodic television rely heavily on clicks. By using the digital metronome, a conductor is able to concentrate on the performance of the orchestra while knowing that the music will be metrically perfect in relation to the picture. A conductor does not want to have to rerecord a good performance because the music is slightly over or under length.

A major challenge for composers who rely on clicks, is to prevent the score from sounding too stilted or metrically uninteresting. Cues can be written with indication for the clicks to be started and stopped, changed, and restarted; or an optical click track can be built to effect an *accelerando* within any piece of music, giving it a tempo diversification. Varying the meter of bars is one way to avoid the repetitive feeling of a too consistent down beat.

When a liberal time schedule exists for a feature film scoring session, the need for reliance on clicks will diminish. However, this certainly does not rule them out or negate their value.

VIDEO METRONOMIC CLICKS

When dealing with video, the creating of variable clicks is extraordinarily precise. If a composer wants to be on a down beat at any given point within a cue, computerized equipment such as the Streamline System will enable the number of bars and beats to be calculated in a division of one one-hundredth of a second. This is much more versatile than the division of one-eighth of a frame. The specifications for a click track can now be programmed by a computer, relieving the music editor of the complicated mathematics necessary to calculate *accelerandos* and *ritardandos*. Once the computer is programmed with the information supplied by the composer's sketch, the computer will record the clicks onto the videotape. The SMPTE time code and the clicks on the videotape can now be transferred either in advance or simultaneously to the recording tape. The videotape, the recording tape, and the picture can be interlocked so that everything can be playing at the same time.

Innovative computer programs with new hardware are being developed faster than the composers or music editors can keep up with them. The most popular new systems, the Spellbinder-Streamline, the Cue System, and the Auricle, were described earlier (see the section on music editing systems for videotape). All allow more precise and diversified musical arrangements than are possible with film technology and simpler metronomes.

THE DOWN BEAT

A down beat does not necessarily indicate the first note of music to be heard. The bar may start with a silent down beat, and the music may then enter on the second, third, or fourth beat of the bar. The term *down beat* is used loosely by composers, musicians, and music editors to indicate the first beat of the first bar of music. In reality, however, it is the first beat of any bar. When a contractor puts out a call for musicians, they ask, "What time's the down beat?" If it's a 9:00 A.M. call, the musicians know they have to be in their places, warmed up, and ready to play at that time.

UNION REGULATIONS

On the scoring session, the music contractor keeps a log of each cue's recording time, calls the rest breaks (ten minutes every hour), issues the forms for payment, marks the doubles for the players, and maintains order on the stage.

The musicians' union contract with the producers' association stipulates a minimum three-hour musician call for any scoring session. The agreement further stipulates, for television scoring, a limit of 15 minutes of recorded music per three-hour session (5 minutes per hour.) If 20 minutes of recorded music is needed, the music contractor will specify a four-hour musician call. The scoring session may be completed in less time, but the orchestra members will be paid for the full four hours. There is no such time stipulation for the scoring of a feature film.

Of the musicians called by the contractor for a scoring session, some are capable of playing more than one instrument. This is especially true of the members of the woodwind, brass, and percussion sections.

Composers have much greater flexibility with orchestral arrangements if they know players can double with different instruments. They can write a happy cue requiring an ocarina to play a lilting melodic line, and then write a cue with a melancholy lead for a bass flute, while knowing that one musician can play either instrument with equal dexterity. The trumpeter playing the main title *doubles* when asked to play a flugelhorn for a romantic cue, and then doubles again when asked to play a cornet for a dance band cue. A keyboard person, after playing an acoustic piano, doubles when asked to play a harpsichord for another cue. The percussion section has the greatest potential for doubles. A percussionist might be asked to play everthing and anything that can make a musical sound by hitting it, rubbing it, twirling it, or throwing it on the floor. In one three-hour session, percussionists could play timpani, gong, bells, chimes, belltree, water bucket, vibraphone, xylophone, marimba, bongos, triangle, cymbals, bull roar, flowerpot, and sit-down drums. Every additional instrument played is considered a double.

The musician's rate of pay for instrumental doubling is regulated by a union pay scale formula, which currently calls for a bonus of 50 percent of their scheduled pay rate for the first double and drops to 20 percent for each additional doubling. The term *double* should not be confused with the obvious *double scale*, which is paid to certain privileged members of the orchestra for their specialized individual musical talents. The contractor also takes care of the arrangements for the rental and cartage of any special musical equipment.

· 10 ·

The Dub
Down Stage

WHEN TO USE A DUB DOWN

When that big refrigerator door slams shut as the last musician exits the scoring stage, the composer and music engineer are left with a 24-, 32-, or 48-multitrack recording, either analog or digital, of the entire score.

Originally, a scoring session would be recorded onto a single-stripe piece of optical negative. Using a microphone identical to the one set up for the instrumental sections today, the music engineer would balance the orchestra and record to a single-channel optical track. Then, unless the engineer got it right the first time, the orchestra would have to return and rerecord the cue. Everyone would have to wait for the laboratory to develop and print the negative in order to hear what had been recorded. There was no such operation as a dub down.

Then tape came into existence as a recording format. Experimentation took place by recording to a single-channel quarter-inch tape. The improved quality of the sound and the economy of the tape led to the expansion of developmental possibilities. The rapid development of quarter-inch stereo, then of half-inch four-track, one-inch eight-track, and ultimately two-inch 16-track, allowed the industry greater diversification and flexibility for increased control of recorded sound. This 16-channel track was the mainstay of the recording industry until the two-inch 24-track recorded was developed, which slowly phased out the 16-track into obsolescence.

In keeping with the truism that change is the only certainty, we now have digital sound recording with a one-inch 32-channel Mitsubishi; the competition is a Sony half-inch tape with 48 channels. Regardless of the recording machine being used, if the number of recorded tracks exceeds six, then a dub down is normally necessary.

THE DUB DOWN

In its simplest form, a dub down is the mixing or blending together of recorded tracks from a greater to a lesser number. This usually takes place immediately after the score is completed. The multitrack recorder containing all the original stage recording is connected to another recording machine for the dub down. Again, the music engineer has complete control over the volume, ambience, and tonality of these tracks. Under the composer's supervision, all the recorded cues are dubbed down to a format requested by the production company. The requested format could consist of a single channel, stereo, three-channel, or four- or six-channel, any of which will be transferred to a 35 mm full-coat for the rerecording or sweetening stage, also referred to as the dubbing stage. It is at this point that the music recordings are polished and mixed with other sounds to create the finished production sound tracks.

Normally, the composer, sitting with the music engineer, listens to the original multitrack as the music engineer has recorded it. While reading the score, the composer makes notes of any sections that should be changed.

The engineer is directed to raise or lower the sound volume and adjust the tonality of the instruments. After a given number of rehearsals by the music engineer and a satisfactory run-through, the cue is ready to be transferred to another format. If the music mixer is fortunate enough to be working with a computerized board, the satisfactory rehearsal will be duplicated by the computer without the need for the mixer to change a setting.

The dub down can take many different forms. The basic format consists of dubbing down to a half-inch four-channel tape. The music engineer assigns the string section to the first channel, the percussion and keyboards to the second, and the brass section to the third. The fourth channel always contains the sync reference.

To avoid a generation loss during a dub down of analog recording, the music can be simultaneously recorded to a 35 mm full-coat and to the half-inch four-track tape. The half-inch tape acts as a protection copy for any additional prints that might be needed. When a dub down to 35 full-coat is not made simultaneously, the dubbed-down cues on the half-inch four-channel tape are transferred to a full-coat 35 mm three-channel tape at a later time. There is no need to transfer the fourth track of the half-inch tape containing the sync reference, as the 35 mm sound recorder dummy always runs at a consistent 24 frames per second.

Another option when scoring is taking place is to record simultaneously on both multitrack and a half-inch four-track tape. With this arrangement, after the scoring session is finished, the composer enters the control booth and listens to all the cues from the half-inch four-channel tape. If the music mix on the half-inch tape meets with the composer's approval, then no further dub down is necessary. If the composer has reservations about the music mix on a particular cue, then the multitrack will be used to dub down and make a new mix. This multitrack is a protection not only for the composer and the engineer but also for the producer and the director, who might ask for a different mix of a cue when they hear it with the sound effects on the final dubbing stage. When a request of this nature is made, the music engineer will return to the scoring stage control booth and, from the multitrack, make a new dub down of that cue with the changes requested by the director or producer. This new dub down will be given to the music editor, who will cut it into the music unit to replace the original cue.

The final dub down mix of the film or video is formatted to the specifications of the film or videotape production department. The sound track for the final dubbing stage can be the entire orchestra blended to a single channel, a three-channel with isolated orchestra sections, a two-channel stereo, or a four- or six-channel stereo. Regardless of the format, the dub down should be as dry as possible. The term dry here refers to the amount of reverberation added to the recording of the instruments. For any film or television project, there is some given amount of indigenous reverberation on the tracks from the ambience of the recording stage. Any additional reverberation is added on the final dubbing stage and not incorporated into the dub down itself. It is better to add this touch on the final dubbing stage, where control of the amount of reverberation will depend on the scene, rather than to have it built into the music, where it cannot be reduced. Reverberation is a matter of aesthetics in the final dubbing of the picture, and the dubbing mixer needs all the options available to integrate the music properly with the dialogue and sound effects. Permanently locking reverberation into the music tracks would place the music mixer on the dubbing stage in an untenable position.

When the dub down of the cues in the score is completed, a 35 full-coat, in the requested format, is delivered to the music editor. This full-coat could be a single-channel, left and right stereo, three-channel, four-channel, or six-channel track. Regardless of the format, the procedure for preparing this track for the final dubbing stage will be the same. The three-track isolated-channels tape was the industry favorite for many years until stereo recording, with its increased potential, became available.

A STEREO DUB DOWN

A stereo dub down consists of blending the orchestra in such a way that there is no individual control of sections or instruments but, rather, a rich, full orchestral sound. Regular stereo recording uses two tracks, with each track routed to a speaker or set of speakers. By distributing different instruments or sections between these tracks, the final sound recreates the relative positions of these sections on the recording stage. Stereo instills in the sound a sense of space. The music engineer might make a clear designation for putting the trumpets on the left channel, having the trombones on the right, and splitting the strings under both. The percussion section could be divided in the same manner. If the dub down stereo mix is to accomplish the correct sound, that format is incongruent to the needs of the final dubbing mixer. Neither the trumpets nor trombones can be raised or lowered without the strings and the percussion increasing and decreasing along with them. The point is that on the final dubbing stage the music mixer has no choice but to raise or lower the entire music cue, without the flexibility of sectional orchestral discernment.

SURROUND SOUND

In some exclusive first-run theaters, stereo has been expanded to a surround sound system: right, left, center, and surround speaker system. This four-speaker structure provides even greater depth than normal two-speaker stereo. When this format is requested by the production company, the music engineer will dub down the multitrack to six channels. There might be a track assignment that would place the strings on tracks 1 and 4, the brass and woodwinds on 2 and 5, and the percussion and lead instruments on 3 and 6. Another option would be a stereo of the orchestra, a stereo of the electronic instruments, and the lead instruments of both isolated on the remaining tracks. A stereo six-channel dub down can be recorded on one eight-track tape while a 35 full-coat six-channel is being made simultaneously.

In ordering the recording machines for a scoring session, there are any number of alternatives that are available to the producer to acquire the necessary tracks for the final dubbing or sweetening stage.

The options that present themselves are as follows:

1. No dub down at all. The scoring session can be recorded directly to:
   a. Quarter-inch monaural tape with sync on second track
   b. Quarter-inch stereo tape with sync in center track
   c. Half-inch four-channel tape for either single, stereo, or three-channel recording (four-channel sync)
   d. 35 single-stripe magnetic film
   e. 35 full-coat with two- or three-channel isolation
   f. 35 full-coat with six-channel isolation
2. Analog multitracks:
   a. Two-inch 16-track
   b. Two-inch 24-track
3. Digital multitracks:
   a. One-inch 32-track
   b. Half-inch 48-track

4. Any of the above will have to be ordered either non-Dolby, Dolby A, or Dolby SR.

Dolby is the name of the engineer who developed a noise reduction system for sound recordings. The Dolby A system divides and monitors the sound spectrum into four sections for the elimination of extraneous noise, whereas the SR system further sophisticates this spectrum into 16 sections. Knowledgeable people who work with sound consistently feel that Dolby SR is "easier listening" than the sterile sound of a digital recording. Perhaps one cannot be too thin or too rich, but it seems that digital sound can be too clean and too pure.

It cannot be said that every multitrack tape must be dubbed down, as there are rare occasions when the multitrack itself is taken to the final dubbing stage. There the music engineer will mix the multitrack directly into the final dub track. This is unusual, but it does happen.

When, for economic reasons, a scoring session is recorded directly to either a half-inch four-track tape, or 35 full-coat three-channel, with no plan for a dub down, the normal mix on the four-track will have the strings on track 1, percussion on track 2, the brass on track 3, and a sync reference on the fourth channel. The 35 full-coat needs no reference, as it runs consistently on sprockets at 24 frames per second. If the composer wants to bring up the lead violin from the body of the string section assigned to channel 1, this is not possible because the strings are locked together. If this cue had been recorded on a 16-, 24-, 32-, or 48-track recorder, then the music engineer, during the dub down, could raise the volume of the isolated lead violin and satisfy the composer's request.

ALBUM DUB DOWN

An additional dub down, separate from the film or video dub down, takes place when there is a request for a commercial album of the entire score. This dub down takes an entirely different approach toward orchestral placement and instrumental blending. The dub down of a score for a record album will usually be recorded to a stereo two-track tape. There will be no isolation of the orchestra sections but, rather, a full, rich blending, with instruments delicately balanced on the two tracks to obtain the most effective stereo sound possible. The composer and the music engineer will add all the flourishes of reverberation and stand-out instrumentation possible to make as enjoyable and as salable a commercial recording as they can. A recording of a film score has no relation to the dialogue or sound effects contained in the picture. It is a pure recording, without regard for anything but the best possible rendition of the music. Reverberation is added, instrumentation is brightened, lead instruments are featured, and the music cues are arranged on the record or compact disc in the most diverse and enjoyable sequences.

· 11 ·

Preparation
for Rerecording
or Sweetening

GETTING IT ALL TOGETHER

In preparing the music from the scoring stage for the final rerecording, when working with film, the first operation is to break
down the music cues from the scoring session. The cues are delivered to the music editor in thousand-foot rolls of 35 mm magnetic film, with tabs identifying the start of each cue. These must be
separated (broken down) into individual rolls. When this operation
is complete, the black-and-white dupe picture and track are
threaded either on a flatbed or on an upright moviola, both of
which should have two sound heads, one for the dialogue track and
the other for the music. At this point the music editor has the black-
and-white dupe picture, the rolls of magnetic film containing the
music tracks, and reels of magnetic film containing the production
dialogue track. After he has broken down the cues, the music editor
must assemble them into new full reels (music units) that are
synchronized with the picture and dialogue.

BUILDING UNITS

To build a music unit, you must have a reel of 35 mm film leader. Film leader is usually an old print of a television series or a long-past film feature; these rolls of film are purchased from a film salvage company. A start mark is placed on this leader in sync with the start mark of the picture and dialogue track. The three reels are run down on the moviola (Figure 11.1) to the footage where the first piece of music is to be heard in the picture. As noted, the

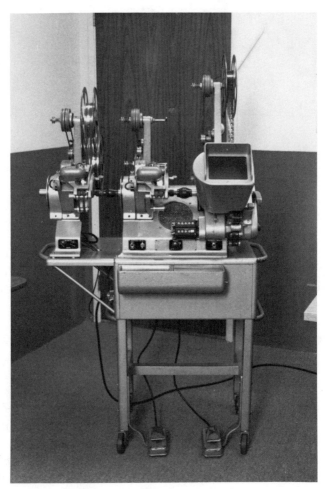

Figure 11.1 A moviola.

recorded music from the scoring stage is on a roll of magnetic film. Every piece of film has two sides, the celluloid side, which is always shiny, and an emulsion side, which carries the picture images. Magnetic film has a celluloid side, but what would be the emulsion side is coated with magnetic tape that holds the recorded sound. The first music cue is run wild (without picture) on the moviola to locate and mark the entrance and exit of the music. This also works as a sound check to ensure there are no "wows" (sound distortion created by change in speed of transfer), cutouts, or bad sound in the transfer.

The cue is then cut into (joined to) the unit with the magnetic side running with the celluloid side of the leader. When building sound into a unit, whether it is dialogue, sound effects, or music, the leader that is going to run against the sound-reproducing head should always be the celluloid side. Emulsion on any film or leader is soft, and if it is run against the reproducing sound heads, the emulsion will rub off on the heads, resulting in a very muffled sound.

When this magnetic track containing the music is properly cut into the unit, all three elements—the picture, the dialogue track, and the music unit—are run in sync with one another on the moviola. The position of the music with respect to the picture and dialogue is carefully checked to ensure that everything is as it should be. Minor adjustments can be made by moving the entire track forward or backward at this time. In the extreme case, the music cue can be cut down or lengthened by the editor to fit the picture more precisely.

As the music is being placed into the unit, the footage and frame of the music's entrance and disappearance must be written in on the mixer's rerecording log. This is an elongated piece of paper with space for the footage and an area to identify what it contains— for example, "Reel 1, music unit 1, Cue 1M1, music starts at 55 feet + 10 frames and ends at 236 feet. It is a three-channel, with stereo orchestra on tracks 1 and 3, vocal only on track 2, recorded Dolby SR." This information tells the mixer the reel and unit number, the footage for the entrance and exit of the music, the position of the orchestra and vocal on the music channels, and the noise reduction used (Dolby SR). Other helpful notes may be included: "Ease in, preset for shock entrance, reverberate ending, and cross-fade to music unit 2 at a given footage. This building continues until all of the recorded cues are integrated into the units."

This integration of scored cues into music units is not difficult. However, the scheduling of the scoring session and the final rerecording is usually so tight that the building of these units falls under great time pressure. In episodic television scoring is done on Monday and rerecording on Tuesday. In extreme instances scoring is done on the same day as rerecording. I'm sure someone, somewhere is working on a plan for being able to score the day after the rerecording.

SOURCE MUSIC

All the cues scored by the composer are tailored to fit the action, dialogue, and mood of the scene. The music cues have been checked by the director and the producer on the scoring stage, so there are no surprises in store for them. But what about the source music? Source music is the bane of a music editor's existence. In case you have forgotten, *source music* emanates from any mechanical source: radios, juke boxes, television sets, Muzak in elevators or shopping centers, live orchestras, organ grinders, calliopes, street singers, to say nothing of boom boxes, record players, and one-man bands. Source music plays over scenes in elevators, night clubs, restaurants, bars, parties, car radios, parks, merry-go-rounds, and the like.

Selecting source music can be the prerogative of the music supervisor, the associate producer, the music editor, or someone only marginally involved in the production.

In our hypothetical, and perhaps fantastic, scenario, the producer has listened and approved the three source tunes he wants to hear over the party sequence. The music editor now has choices to make. Regardless of the producer's approval, the music editor is faced with decisions about the placement of these selections. Which tune should be playing when we cut to the party? Should the first tune be heard on the exterior of the house, or will we just hear it when we cut inside? Either way, should it be already playing (in progress) or start at the top?

If the music editor is fortunate enough to have a definitive opinion, then she should go with it. A music editor should cut songs in the way she feels they should be and hope for the best. The director or producer will invariably want to play with them to see if one tune doesn't work better over the ending than another, or to try starting with the one that is now in the middle and putting the middle one at the end. Perhaps they sounded just fine on the cassette, but against the dialogue they don't work, so all three tunes will be changed from hard rock to soft jazz. There is no way that source music can be positioned in a sequence with any assurance that it will stay that way.

THE VIDEO PRELAY STAGE

For a film dubbing stage, music cues are built into film units that run on sound dummies in sync with the picture. For a video production, instead of building music units, the music is transferred to a multitrack tape on a prelay stage.

When music is recorded on the scoring stage to a video program, the SMPTE time code numbers are regenerated from the videotape directly to one of the channels of the recording multitrack tape. The music engineer on the scoring stage will have dubbed down, or directly recorded, to a four-channel half-inch tape. The first three channels contain the music, and the fourth channel carries the SMPTE code of the video picture for which the music was recorded. This SMPTE time code interlocks that music with a segment of the video picture.

The music editor will take the dubbed-down half-inch tape from the scoring session to a prelay room, which contains a video monitor, a small mixing panel, a half-inch machine, and a multitrack (24-, 32-, or 48-track) recorder. The multirack is striped with the SMPTE time code of the complete video program on the last channel. The SMPTE code on the half-inch music track will interlock with the SMPTE time code of the multitrack to position the music correctly in a pictorial sense.

The music editor will sit with the engineer at the prelay panel and, with the half-inch music track, together they will prelay the three music tracks onto three tracks of the multitrack in the corresponding areas of the video program. As the half-inch music track already contains the SMPTE time code as an absolute sync, this prelay is an expeditious process.

The situation is not the same when the music has been either scored to film or recorded wild (to timings and clicks only). In this case, there is no compatible SMPTE time code to align the recorded music to the prestriped multitrack tape. The music will have to be rolled in by stopping the video at the spot where the music cue will start, then locating the start of the music on the half-inch tape, interlocking the two, backing up for a preroll to allow sufficient startup time, activating the machines simultaneously, and recording the music onto the multitrack.

The cues on the prelay multitrack are complete as scored, and any overlaps or segues will be placed on additional tracks with no attempt to fade in or out, just a straight transfer as the music has been recorded or dubbed down on the half-inch. The usual number of tracks taken by the music is six. Music cues and track assignments are noted individually on a sweetening log that indicates the cue number, the SMPTE time code start and end of the cue, and the material on each track—strings on track 22, percussion on track 21, brass on track 20, and so on. Track 23 is left void, as track 24 will carry the SMPTE time code and the empty channel 23 will ensure that there is no leakage of that code onto the music channel. The remainder of the channels on the multitrack will be used by the sound effects editors to prelay their dialogue, Foley, and ADR tracks, in some instances syncing to the SMPTE time code, and in others rolling in effects in the same manner as the non-SMPTE music tracks. An entire production, from start to finish, can be assembled without ever touching a piece of film.

The entire purpose of the prelay operation is to eliminate time on the sweetening stage, where all the elements, dialogue, effects, and Foley, are combined. With the prelay system, all elements are in proper position and in sync with the picture and are contained on one or more multitracks.

THE SWEETENING STAGE

The sweetening stage is an offshoot of the film dubbing stage and, in Hollywood, uses three mixers: one for dialogue, one for music, and one for effects.

The difference between a sweetening stage and a dubbing stage is in the loading room equipment. The dubbing stage has long banks of sound dummies that are loaded with reels of film containing the dialogue, sound effects, and music all in sync with the picture. The sweetening stage (Figure 11.2) will have two or possibly three multitrack machines that replace all the sound dummies found on a dubbing stage. The mixer's panel has different equipment for controlling the offsets required occasionally for track adjustments, but only the electronics differ, not the function.

There is no difference in the end product, whether it be video or film. The results are the same: a composite or stereo track of dialogue, effects, and music blended to the producer's satisfaction.

SOUND EFFECTS AND DIALOGUE

The music editor and the sound effects editors usually start on a project at about the same time. In more than a few instances, the spotting of music will take place at the same time as the spotting for sound effects. This is not an ideal situation, but it happens nevertheless. Credit should be given to the people whose work makes the dialogue audible and the effects realistic. The sound

Figure 11.2 Equipment for video playback and recording on the scoring stage.

effects editors, in many ways, are not appreciated as they should be. When you hear a door close and the latch snap shut, in a movie, you don't think anything about it—it's a natural sound and you expect it. But there isn't a door on a shooting set in Hollywood with a catch, latch, or lock, as they would make noise and could jam, complicating an actor's entry or exit. No one thinks twice about a sound that's inherent to the action, but I can remember seeing a foreign film where a window shade was pulled down and then released but there was no sound for the flapping of the shade. The absence of sound immediately dismissed any vicarious identification and diminished the enjoyability of the story.

The preparation of dialogue, sound effects, and music units is a meticulous operation for everyone concerned.

A scene of a person walking to a car, getting in, and driving away may consist of seven or more separate units: a unit with a track of the footsteps and body movements (Foley) (see Figure 11.3), a track for the car door opening, one for the door closing, another for the car starting, a track for the sound of the engine as the car pulls away, a track for the tire squealing, and a traffic background

Figure 11.3 The Foley stage, with its various surfaces and sound makers. The operator literally watches the screen and makes the required shoe-scuffing-on-heavy-gravel or key-turning-in-rusty-lock noises.

track. If it's a night scene, the editor will make a cricket loop (a tape or program designed to repeat a sound indefinitely); if it's daytime, there will be a bird loop and a light wind loop. They might throw in a distant train or a dog barking in the distance. This is to say nothing of the dialogue track. If, on the shooting set, the recordist was not in a position to record dialogue lines as clearly as they should be, the dialogue is duplicated on the ADR stage and there could be several readings of one line. These options, as well as the original dialogue, will be running at the same time so the director can make a definitive decision as to which reading is the better. If the sounds and dialogue are not properly isolated on individual units for volume control, it is very difficult for the mixer to achieve the delicate balance required. For example, the dog might sound as if it is in the car instead of three blocks away.

Each editor has the responsibility for constructing the units so that there is enough isolation between the different sound entrances to give the rerecording mixer time to adjust the volume control for the next sound effect on that unit.

· 12 ·

The Rerecording and Sweetening Stage

THE STAGE

Although termed the *rerecording stage*, in film vernacular this facility is not really a stage at all but rather a projection room with an elaborate mixing panel connected to sound reproducers and elaborate recording equipment (see Figure 12.1). This room is also called the dubbing stage or the mixing stage. In video terms, the room that functions in an identical manner is referred to as a *sweetening stage*.

Either the rerecording or the sweetening stage is the room where a mixer or mixers polish and combine every sound element for a production. In the rerecording room, the first thing that strikes the eye is the elongated mixing board containing all the necessary dials, levers, switches, knobs, patch cords, panels, and other controls that enable the mixers to have complete command over every sound the editorial staff supplies. Outside of this mixing board, there is little to differentiate this room from any other projection room. A projectionist, recordist, and loader, respectively, operate the visual and sound equipment in the rerecording

Figure 12.1a The rerecording room. Notice the viewing screen and Ping-Pong table.

Figure 12.1b Patching cables. Back panel of rerecording stage.

Figure 12.1c A recording panel for 35 mm film on scoring stage. Used primarily for dub down recording.

room. Some rooms contain a few couches and plush chairs, some recreational equipment, a Ping-Pong table, and/or a pool table.

The *loading room*, usually located immediately behind the rerecording room, is the place where all the heavy equipment is located (Figure 12.2). There might be 40 dummies (nonrecording sound reproducers) on which the sound units are loaded. The sound editors deliver all of their units to the loading room and each unit is assigned a specific dummy. The individual who manages this part of the operation is a *loader*. The sound effects editor will invariably have supplied many more units to the stage than the dialogue, ADR, or music editor. The mixer is notified of each of these units and assigns one of the volume control levers on the mixing board to that unit. Then the volume, timbre, reverb, speaker location, and other aural characteristics can be controlled by the mixer.

THE HOLLYWOOD SYSTEM

The advent of sound in motion picutres necessitated the use of mixers to rerecord the dialogue, sound effects, and music into one sound track. The units consisted of sounds photographed on opti-

Figure 12.2 The loading room, often found directly behind the rerecording room.

cal film, and the rerecording of these sounds was to an optical negative. If the mixer made a mistake when rerecording to optical, he couldn't back up as one does nowadays with magnetic tape. He had to throw the negative away and start over. There was just one pass, straight through, with no stops—and it had to be right. That's why the movie industry developed the three-person mixing panel, called the *Hollywood system.* It was impossible for one person to concentrate on all three elements at the same time without something suffering in the rerecording. The movie industry has never been one for featherbedding in the work force; these positions evolved out of necessity.

When magnetic tape came into the industry, it revolutionized the recording and rerecording of films. The availability of forward and reverse action, which allowed erasing and recording over any section of a project, brought about a better and more sophisticated product. However, the three-person crew remained, and to this day there is no thought of changing this arrangement. The extra attention to detail and the ability to specialize allowed by the Hollywood system help produce a top-quality sound, even given the advantages of multitrack. These positions are held by highly qualified, talented, and respected individuals.

The rerecording mixers on a standard rerecording stage in Hollywood work together as individual specialists on the rerecording panel. The mixer who handles the dialogue and ADR tracks is considered the head of the panel. Of the other two mixers, one specializes in sound effects and the other specializes in music. The three work together to satisfy the producer or director regarding the proper levels and sophistication of the sounds supplied by the editors. The producer and various sound and music editors normally attend the rerecording session, the former to give approval, and both to offer input and contribute to a successful and efficient session. Having three mixers on a rerecording panel, each with expertise attuned to his individual specialty, permits all the elements to be run at the same time, which would be difficult if one person were operating the entire board. The Hollywood system allows the producer to obtain a proper impression immediately. It also results in a much shorter rerecording session. These are the strong points in favor of the Hollywood system.

THE NEW YORK SYSTEM

New York has a small but steady feature film industry. However, the mainstay of the New York industry is in the production of commercials. For a film scoring session in New York, it is impossible to get the best orchestra players for a morning down beat; they are all booked solid recording television commercials. These commercials, like all films and videotape productions, must be rerecorded. In the many and varied rerecording rooms in New York, there is always just one person on the mixing panel, handling the narration, dialogue, sound effects, and music. In most instances, one individual can rerecord a 60-second commercial in a day's time to the satisfaction of the client. However, the one-mixer system called the *New York system*, has become so ingrained that there is no flexibility in catering to the Hollywood producer who rerecords a feature in New York and requests a three-person mixing panel.

For a feature film, the New York system, with one person doing all the mixing on the rerecording panel, is ludicrous. The mixer first rerecords the dialogue tracks for the entire picture (the average time is one reel per day). This dialogue track may be perfectly audible, but when the sound effects are added in the second phase of the rerecording (another reel per day), some dialogue will have to be rebalanced, as it is now nearly obliterated by the sound effects. The third and final step is adding the music (two to three reels per day). Again, this necessitates the rebalancing of sound effects and dialogue.

It is impossible for a music editor to be kind, understanding, or even pleasant while rerecording a feature in New York. The music, as the last item to be added, suffers ignominy under this system. The mixer has first concentrated on the dialogue, then worked with the sound effects, and then—almost as an afterthought—added the music. None of the elements gets a fair shake and the mix invariably turns out "vanilla"; that is, the dynamics suffer, and everything—dialogue, sound effects, and music—is bland. This is not the mixer's fault, but rather the nature of the operation. It's difficult to play a hand of cribbage, then switch to bridge, and end up in a poker game without losing some of your concentration.

If one subscribes to the adage that time is money—and on the rerecording stage it certainly is—then the New York system is the more expensive of the two. The time taken to rerecord is at least tripled, and so are the rerecording charges. The money saved by not using two extra mixers is absorbed by the stage rental as well as the salaries paid to the loader, recordist, and projectionist for the necessary additional time. Another expense is for editorial personnel, who are contractually committed to stay on salary until the completion of the rerecording. And let us not discount the producer's valuable time. It would seem, from this perspective, that the primary justification for a producer to use a one-person rerecording operation would be the convenience of the locale.

There are, however, situations in which the New York system can be very effective. Generally this is true when scheduling pressures are not extreme. *Apocalypse Now*, which deservedly won an Oscar for Best Sound, was mixed in San Francisco by one man. If you analyze the diverse and creative sounds that enfold in the opening reel of that epic film, you can easily understand the immense amount of time (over a year) and effort that went into the final rerecording of this picture to make it an outstanding work of sound artistry.

THE RERECORDING

In this era of specialization, rerecording mixers are among the most highly skilled people in our business. They do amazing things in filtering noisy dialogue tracks or telephone conversations, adding reverberation, removing sibilance, affecting perspective, removing highs or lows, and performing other innovative tasks to make the sound cleaner, more realistic, or dramatically different.

Music, on the other hand, is not a natural embellishment. It is the only foreign element in the film and, as such, has to be handled with sensitivity. The person who sits in the music mixer's chair must have a good musical ear and a refined sense of drama. To have the privilege of working with the best mixers, to hear the music swell and decrease with the emotions of a scene, gives one an appreciation for both the mixer and the composer.

The mixers are there for one purpose only, and that is to rerecord the film the way the producer or director wants it to sound. The rerecording stage has a large footage counter located below the projection screen. The mixers, watching this counter and following the footages written on the rerecording logs, will adjust their levels to the entrances of the dialogue, sound effects, and music, and cut in at those footages. They integrate those sounds into a predetermined format of monaural, stereo, or surround sound, giving a fullness and realism to otherwise mundane scenes.

The mixers will do everything possible to achieve the quality and balance of sound requested by a producer, but they will not allow anyone actually to manipulate the dials on the panel. The mixers know better than anyone else what they can and cannot do with the electronics available to them on the mixing panel. For a producer, director, composer, sound effects editor, or music editor to infiltrate the mixing panel would be ill advised (aesthetics aside, they also have a strong union).

STEREO RERECORDING

Time spent on the rerecording stage is expensive, and the common practice of making stereo and surround sound tracks lengthens the time element. The swinging of sounds from one speaker to another and the placement of sounds compound the efforts of the rerecording mixers. In addition, there is the rental of highly technical equipment and the acquisition of permits and *cards* (transistor boards) from the Dolby sound system.

For stereo rerecordings, the mixers need the dialogue, sound effects, and music units prepared so that the sounds can be easily assigned to the correct speaker. This makes extra work for the sound effects editor and necessitates the utilization of many more units. The sound of a car driving by will require the mixer to swing the sound from the speaker on the left to the one on the right. Each actor's dialogue lines must be cut into a unit for the appropriate speaker in relationship to their location on the screen. The music units take many different forms. Some are three-channel, with hard assignments of orchestra sections—strings on channel 1, percussion on 2, and brass on 3. With this arrangement, the rerecording mixer may arrange the sounds for different speakers to effect a stereo mix with the ultimate in volume control.

The arrangement of isolated-track instrumentation gives the music mixer on the final rerecording stage the greatest possible flexibility in controlling the volume of the instrumental sections. There are many important reasons for this orchestral separation. The string section alone can be reverberated without the percussion and brass sections being affected. Any one track, or all three, can be sweetened in this fashion without the other tracks swimming all over the score. If a producer or director on the final rerecording stage feels the music is stepping on dialogue, instead of having to lower the entire cue—or, worse yet, drop it entirely—the music rerecording mixer can lower the brass or percussion channels without decreasing the volume of the strings and thereby maintain the essence of the cue.

The composer is concerned with the best possible rendition of the orchestra and has usually written around the dialogue so that this is not something that happens too often. The flexibility of control over the three channels gives the rerecording mixer additional options for overcoming unforeseen circumstances that arise consistently on the final rerecording stage. For example, there could be a new sound integrated into the sound effect track for the final rerecording, of which the composer was not informed, but which now conflicts with the music. Or there could be additional dialogue lines or new narration, all of which would affect the musical score or the positioning of the music. The cue might have too much movement in the percussion section for the pacing of the scene, in which case the percussion track could be dropped.

The most common format today is a premixed stereo on six channels that the composer has supervised, and the function of the mixer is in volume control and speaker assignment. The entire orchestra has been premixed, so there are no isolated instruments that the mixer can feature or reduce in volume. This guarantees the composer that the music will be heard as it was designed, or not heard at all, as the rerecording mixer will have no control of the orchestral sections. The mixer's main function is the proper assignment of the six-channel stereo tracks to the best perspective. This arrangement lessens the creativity of the music rerecording mixer in the area of orchestral control but adds the complexities of assigning six tracks to the speakers in a stereo surround environment.

Regardless of the rerecording expense, more and more product is being dubbed in stereo. In the developmental stage of videotape, stereo capabilities were included as an integral part of the sound format. The capabilities of stereo sound for television programs has influenced many producers to change the format of their rerecording from monaural to stereo, if only in preparation for the time when all programs will be transmitted in stereo.

THE PRODUCER AT THE RERECORDING

On the rerecording stage, the producer is hearing the music for the second time. The first time, which occurred when the music was being recorded on the scoring stage, afforded him an excellent opportunity to perceive the effect of the music on the scene. However, the music cues are recorded out of context and not in the order in which they will be heard during a screening (usually full orchestra cues first), and this gives an out-of-context impression.

Thematic material may become too repetitive as the picture progresses: "It sounded good on the scoring stage, but I can't stand to hear that 'du bee du bee du' one more time." Or an added optical *camera move in* that was not integrated into the picture when the spotting took place may now beg for music.

The music editor is always present on the rerecording stage to make any changes or adjustments requested by the producer. Music is shortened, lengthened, thrown out, moved to different places, all at the producer's demand. The music editor, who is being paid by the producer, is there to ensure that the producer's requests are satisfied and, at the same time, to maintain the thematic integrity of the composer's music.

The reasons for musical changes on the rerecording stage are innumerable. Sometimes they have nothing to do with logic but are based on the personal whim of the producer.

If a producer requests music under a scene that has not been scored, the composer, if present, or the music editors will select a piece of music from within the existing score that will work for that scene. The music editor orders one or two prints (copies) of that cue, and perhaps others to act as alternates, and then makes any necessary edits to tailor the music to fit the new scene. The music editor is the composer's representative on the rerecording stage, and his function is to protect the integrity of the composer's music when changes are requested. The music editor also endeavors to keep the producer from having the music sound apologetic (too low), obtrusive (too loud), or unfinished (dialed out too soon.) If the composer is present on the rerecording stage, the composer and music editor will confer on how best to handle any request made by the producer.

The rerecording or sweetening stage is the frosting on the cake. It is the last creative step available to a producer or director before the picture or videotape program is released to the theaters or appears on television. Anyone who has had anything to do with the filming of a production would, in retrospect, have done some things differently. When the picture is being rerecorded, the mixers continually run the scenes in forward and reverse to perfect the level and tenor of the sounds. All those involved—producers, directors, editors—see their good work, their compromises, their errors in judgment, all playing over and over as the rerecording crew rehearses and rerecords on the rerecording stage.

Anyone can discuss changes with the producer regarding her particular area of expertise. If the requested change is valid, the producer will ask, or allow the editor to ask, a mixer to make that adjustment. The producer will certainly allow a composer or music editor to give direction to the music mixer and will allow the sound effects editor to aid the sound effects mixer.

There is an unwritten rule applying to rerecording room decorum for dialogue, sound effects, and music editors: Do not offer a critique of any area except one's own. Sound effects editors do not discuss the music, and music editors to not comment on the sound effects.

The bottom line remains: Criticism is the prerogative of the producer.

THE COMPOSER AT THE RERECORDING

A composer's contractual agreement with the production company is satisfied upon completion of the scoring session. She has composed, orchestrated, and conducted the score, with no further obligation to attend the final rerecording. But there is a tacit understanding that, if possible, she'll be there. Realistically, the rerecording stage is the only place a composer can evaluate the effectiveness of her musical judgments. Regardless of a composer's credentials, there has never been a score recorded that could not have been changed in some subtle way to improve its relationship to a picture. There are always nuances that might have been handled differently—instrumentation under dialogue, tacit or silent beats to allow for sound effects, tempo changes that would better accentuate the motion, and correction of misjudgments in the spotting session. A composer who follows her music through the final rerecording grows in experience and expertise. It's the best teacher in the industry. In addition, the production usually benefits from having the composer attend the rerecording session. As talented and as familiar with the score as a music editor may be, he is not the person who wrote the music. Musically, no one knows more about the score than the composer.

Unfortunately, composers of episodic television, with its tight time schedule, are usually occupied writing music for the next segment and cannot afford the luxury of spending time on the rerecording stage.

When the composer is present on the final rerecording, changes requested by the producer may result in a confrontation. Some composers will fight for their music; sometimes they'll win and sometimes they'll lose. The result of these skirmishes is always unpredictable and interesting. An uncompromising composer may not be rehired by that producer. Then again, the admiration for someone who cares enough to do battle for his musical interpretation may bring about a respect that builds a lasting relationship.

Axiom #1:	A composer should be on the rerecording stage.
Axiom #2:	The producers will make fewer musical changes if the composer is present.
Axiom #3:	Composers will try to avoid the rerecordings, as it is boring for them when the rerecording crew is not working with the music cues.
Axiom #4:	When musical changes are requested, it is not pleasant for a composer to have to defend her work.
Bottom line:	It's the producer's picture.

THE UNDERSCORE MUSIC

Again, underscore music must be handled in such a way that it does not become the central focus of the audience's attention. The music is there to enhance the emotional value of the film and not to stand on its own. Musical entrances should be unobtrusive, except when shock or heavy drama is part of the emotional impact. Ideally, music will tail out under a dialogue line or a sound effect, so subtly that its disappearance will not be noticed.

There is a saying that if you are aware of the underscore music, then it's wrong. While this is not an adage engraved in stone, there is certainly validity to the statement. The key word is *underscore*. When underscore music triggers an emotional response without diverting the attention of the audience from the drama, then the music is performing its proper function. Main title music played over opening credit cards is certainly not enhancing a scene—it is setting a mood, and you are very much aware of it.

DOMESTIC VERSION

The final rerecording or sweetening of a production (in English) is referred to as the *domestic version*. For a film, all of the material supplied by the dialogue, sound effects, and music editors is rerecorded on a thousand-foot roll of three-, four-, or six-channel 35 mm full-coat magnetic film. In the case of a three-channel rerecording, all the dialogue is assigned to one channel, another channel contains the sound effects, and the remaining channel is for the music. These channels are referred to as the dialogue stem, sound effects stem, and music stem.

Upon completion of the domestic version, these three stems are combined to make a composite track: the dialogue, sound effects, and music, composited and transferred (photographed) to an optical negative. This sound track negative is printed with the picture to make the final release prints that are distributed to theaters in English-speaking countries throughout the world.

FOREIGN VERSION

The domestic release print, with English dialogue, is not acceptable for release in non-English-speaking countries. Rather than rerecording the entire sound track or burning in subtitles for each country interested in exhibiting the film, a system was devised to save the sound effects and music stems, and replace just the English dialogue stem with actors' voices in their native tongue.

In the elimination of the dialogue stem, any sounds that were in the set recordist's original dialogue production tract will be lost. A conversation in a cafe with the clinking of glasses, the movement of the waiter, the sound of water being poured into a glass—all will be eliminated when the dialogue stem is not included in the foreign version (dub). The sound effects editor has the responsibility of examining every original dialogue scene, duplicating the sounds that were inherent in that dialogue track, and supplying the rerecording stage with those additional sound effects units. These units are then blended into the original sound effects stem to make the foreign version dub.

The foreign version dub, when complete, contains two stems: a music stem and a sound effects stem that duplicates every footstep, body motion, and miscellaneous sound that is pictorially or dramatically necessary. There is always the possibility of adding or deleting scenes for the foreign release; in that case, both sound effects and music need changes. The foreign version is basically the transfer of the sound effects and music stems to a roll of 35 mm magnetic full-coat three-channel film. This is referred to as the *M and E track* (music and effects stems). When the M and E track is received in a foreign country, actors on an ADR (automated dialogue replacement) stage will rerecord the translated dialogue in their native tongue. This foreign language dialogue is recorded into the empty dialogue stem, and then all three stems are combined to make a new optical negative that is used to create a new sound track for the picture.

STEREO SOUND IN RELEASE PRINTS

In order to place stereo sound on the *release prints* shown in movie theaters, a special 35 mm film stock with smaller perforations was developed to provide for two optical tracks on the sound track area. This *foxhole perforation stock* has now become the standard for release prints. Sound equipment on projection machines had to be converted to accommodate the two optical Dolby tracks on the release print. The majority of small neighborhood theaters could not afford the expense of converting their equipment to a Dolby sound system with stereo speakers. When a stereo print runs in your local neighborhood theater, the stereo tracks that were so expensive to produce will be heard monaurally because the theater's equipment is not capable of reproducing a stereo sound track.

· 13 ·

Music Report

THE BASIC FORMAT

Upon completion of the rerecording, a music report form is completed by the music editor and sent to the production company. A standard form includes the music cue number, the title of the cue, the name of the composer, the affiliate of the composer (BMI or ASCAP), the name of the publishing company and the publisher's affiliate (BMI or ASCAP), the length of time in minutes and seconds the music cue plays, and the use of that cue in the production.

An example is as follows:

Cue	Title	Composer	Publisher	Time	Usage
1M3	"Flees"	Mary Tune (BMI)	Post-Grad (BMI)	1:34	Score

Cue: 1M3 signifies reel 1 (1)—music (M)—third piece of music in the reel (3).

Cue Title	*Composer*	*Publisher*	*Time*	*Usage*

Title: The composer or music editor titles each cue in reference to the action or dialogue within the scene it is underscoring: "The Rescue," "Bill Burgles," "To the Robbery," and so on.

Composer: The name of the composer and her music society affiliation: ASCAP, BMI, or the foreign society SECAM.

Publisher: The publishing company and its affiliation. Both the composer and the publisher should have the same music affiliation. In the event the production company has apportioned a percentage of its rights to the composer, then both publishing companies are listed, with their percentages of ownership. When there is an equal division, the administration of the account should be specified.

Time: Total length of time the music cue plays in that scene. It is listed in minutes and seconds (1:34).

Usage: There are five categories of usage:

1. *Visual vocal*: A group or individual on screen singing a song
2. *Visual instrumental*: A group or individual on screen playing instruments
3. *Visual source*: Music from a juke box; radio; record, cassette, or CD player; television set; calliope; music box; organ grinder; or other sound source that is visible on screen
4. *Nonvisual source*: Source music that can be heard, but the source of which cannot be seen on screen (Muzak, off-stage radio, etc.)
5. *Underscore*: Original music written by a composer to play under the dramatic scenes.

The music report form must contain every bit of music in the production: the composer's music; any music purchased by the producer for the picture; anything sung, hummed, or whistled; or even dialogue that happens to be a song title or lyrics contained within a song. It will cost the production company dearly if an ad lib line by an actor happens to be a lyric of a popular song.

This report form, which the production company will use for music licensing, cannot be completed until the final rerecording is finished. The changes on the rerecording stage will affect the length, positioning, and number of playings or omission of the music cues. The listing of each music cue in the final rerecording is the last function of the music editor for the production company.

The report form must be submitted to either ASCAP or BMI by the production company for each and every production: feature film, television program, commercial, documentary, cartoon, trailer (coming attractions), and so forth.

This form is used by ASCAP or BMI to credit the music cues to the respective composers and the publishing to the proper companies. The original music is credited to the production company's music publishing company, and any purchased music to the rightful publisher.

ASCAP and BMI need the information contained in the music report to formulate the collection and allocation of monies to the composer and the publisher of the music. Main and end titles, visual vocals, and the like all have varying degrees of percentages when the affiliates determine distribution.

ASCAP AND BMI

There are two organizations in the United States that are responsible for monitoring and collecting monies for music publisher and composer. The first and oldest organization is the American Society of Composers, Authors, and Publishers (ASCAP). ASCAP is completely owned and controlled by its own membership of composers and publishers. The second organization, Broadcast Music Inc. (BMI), was formed at a later time by a group of radio broadcasters and is owned and controlled by a subsidiary corporation of the networks.

A songwriter or screen composer should investigate both organizations to determine which would be preferable for her needs, as these societies have different formulas for the distribution of collected monies. Each individual must make a choice, as one cannot be a member of both. Generally, more songwriters will be found with ASCAP and more screen composers with BMI.

REVENUE AND DISTRIBUTION

The collection and distribution formulas of ASCAP and BMI are extremely complex. Generally, the owners of every jukebox in any public establishment—ice cream parlors, restaurants, bars, and so on—must pay a licensing fee to both BMI and ASCAP to play any song on that jukebox. Songs heard over a radio are monitored, and every broadcasting station pays a fee to ASCAP or BMI for the use of those songs by themselves as entertainment or as part of a production. Obviously, a video or film production pays a fee to use such music in any way. In Europe, this fee extends to television programs and theaters for the film music. These and other sources bring a great deal of revenue to ASCAP or BMI.

As a rough illustration of this payment system, imagine that the monies received from various sources for a song are put into a big pot. A division must be made between the composer(s) and the publisher(s). Assume in this case one-half of all of the publishers and the other half for all of the composers. Now, there are many more composers than there are publishers, so half of the monies reserved for the publishers is shared among fewer components, making the individual publishing sums higher. That is the motivating force behind a composer's request for, or a production company's retention of, the publishing rights. ASCAP and BMI's collection and disbursement service does not include a pot, and the division certainly isn't 50/50.

The foregoing example, of course, is only a very loose interpretation of an extremely complex payment structure.

MUSIC PUBLISHING

When a production company hires a composer to write a score for a production, the company is in fact buying original music from that composer. The composer is selling her music to the production company. What would you do if you owned music that was going to be played in theaters and on television around the world? You would form a music publishing company. Why? Because a music publishing company receives payments from the playing of music in foreign theaters, on the radio, on jukeboxes, and on television.

Forming a music publishing company is easily accomplished by joining not one but both of the affiliates as a publisher.

TWO PUBLISHING COMPANIES

The apportioning of the revenues to be distributed, when a composer has an affiliate that differs from the production company's, is so complex that no equitable payment plan can be found. For this reason, production companies will establish two publishing companies, one with ASCAP and the other with BMI. Thus, a film production company called Post Grad Productions, Inc., will establish one publishing company, University Music, Inc., that will affiliate with ASCAP, and another, College Music, Inc., affiliated with BMI. Both music publishing companies are owned by Post Grad Productions. When a composer is selected to score a production, it does not matter with which society she is affiliated. In either case, Post Grad Productions will list its compatible publishing company. If the composer is affiliated with ASCAP, Post Grad's publishing company will be listed as University Music, Inc. (ASCAP); if she is an affiliate of BMI, then the publishing company will be listed as College Music, Inc. (BMI).

When contract negotiations are in progress, composers should have their agents ask for some percentage, or all, of the music publishing rights on a project. Some production companies will accede to this request; others will not. The reason, of course, is money. If the production company gives away the publishing rights, and the main title song turns out to be a number one hit on the charts, the production company will have lost a good source of additional revenue.

· 14 ·

Tracking

WHY USE TRACKING

When the spotting session for a feature film, "Movie of the Week," or television pilot is completed, the producer might be six weeks away from having the composer's original scored music dubbed into the production. But it is not a viable alternative for the producer to exhibit the project for the heads of the studio or networks, preview audiences, distributors, and other individuals deemed important enough to justify a screening, without some underscore music in the sound track. This requires that music be selected, edited, built into units, and quickly rerecorded to integrate that music into the production sound track. Placing such temporary music into a production is referred to as *tracking*.

The music used in this temporary dub is obtained from many different sources: commercial recordings of film scores, pop recordings, concerts, commercial music libraries, and so on. As long as the project will never be shown or aired commercially, there is no legal problem with compositional or publishing copyright infringement.

DIPLOMACY OF SELECTING MUSIC

Tracking is the art of selecting previously recorded music from commercial recordings of film scores or other music sources, having the music transferred to magnetic 35 mm film, or quarter-inch tape for video, and editing that music to fit the scenes that need to be underscored. The temporary music tracks will be rerecorded with the production track on a rerecording or sweetening stage.

The composer may be writing a score for acoustic instruments, an electronic score, a period classical style, or a contemporary score. The music editor will have to stay within the musical concept of the planned score when selecting music. Budgetary limitations imposed on a composer as to the size of the recording orchestra have to be considered. If a small orchestra is going to be used to underscore the project, the editor can't "temp" track with recordings by the London Philharmonic Orchestra. She also cannot select electronic music if the composer is planning an acoustic score.

When a temp track assignment is given to a music editor, the first item on the agenda is to call the composer who is writing the original score for the production and ask if she has any music from a previous project that she feels will capture the mood of the picture. This is a protective device for both the composer and the editor, as the composer will then have her music in the temporary dub and will not have to compete with another composer's musical style in writing original music for the final score.

When not supplied by the composer, the temporary music has to be selected by the music editor with all of these thoughts in mind. The producer or director might have a film score in mind that he feels would be close to what he would like to hear in the picture. This makes things a little easier, as there is now some direction. The music editor can then proceed with the selection of music cues from the film score recording and supplement that with additional recordings of a similar sound.

SELECTION OF MUSIC

If you are in the position of selecting music for a project, there is only one person to satisfy, and that is yourself. It is impossible to second-guess someone else's emotional concept of a scene. The most considerate decision the music editor can make is to transfer his choice of musical material and some of the other predominant cues to a cassette, play them for the producer, and get her reactions before proceeding with the actual cutting and building of units. People's musical tastes can range from rock to Bach, and if your musical taste is too divergent from the producer's, someone else should be found to complete the project.

There was a time when music editors would track entire episodic television series from prerecorded theme sets. The editors were individually selected for a television series on the basis of their musical tastes. Some action projects need a "hit 'em over the head" approach, with big musical splashes; others require a more subtle approach. Remember, if your musical tastes aren't appreciated by one producer, some other producer may still think you're a genius.

PICKING CUES

Once the composer has furnished the music from past compositions, the music editor goes to work. With the spotting notes in hand (noting the points where music has been requested to underscore), the music is played on a record player, cassette player, or quarter-inch tape machine. While listening to the music, the editor can determine what music is appropriate for a particular scene. This selection process is referred to as picking.

The first selection should be for the main title, as that theme will set the feeling for the entire score. Once the determination of the main title music is made, the orchestral sound and variation on this theme should be carried out with consistency throughout the remainder of the underscore.

To track a show properly, the music editor will use the same spotting or breakdown notes supplied to the composer. The breakdown notes tell the music editor everything he needs to know about the scene and the specific timings of the events within the scene. The most important aspect is the accentuation of the mood.

After reviewing a scene, the editor should play music until a cue or section of a cue is located that complements the mood to be underscored. Starting the cue and the stopwatch on the first note or selected phrase of the music, the music editor, by following both the breakdown notes and the stopwatch timings, can make an immediate determination as to whether the music will work for the scene.

The music does not have to fit perfectly; it can be stretched by intercutting with a second print or trimmed down by editing to hit the cuts and the action within the scene. If the music editor is patient and does not try to rush the picking process, the music editing will be easily accomplished. Any selections that have not been carefully timed or are based on sloppy notes will result in much additional work when editing that selection to fit the scene.

BUILDING THE TEMPORARY TRACKS

The music transfer department of the production company has made reprints on magnetic film of all the selections that have been picked. Now the editing starts. The music units are positioned in the same fashion as they would be in preparation for a final dub. In film, the picture and track are threaded onto a moviola or flatbed and run down to the first scene to be tracked.

In tracking music for a video production, the selected music is transferred to a quarter-inch tape and, using a video prelay room, the music is dubbed onto channel 2 of the three-quarter-inch videotape production. The editing of the quarter-inch music tape in the prelay room, for those who work in 35 mm film, seems tedious, as the tape is delicate and there are no sprocket holes to facilitate splicing. The music is synchronized with the picture and played against this scene. Seldom does the piece of music "lay in"—that is, fit perfectly. Adjustments are made by eliminating musical phrases or shortening held notes. Smooth transitions can be made by placing another print in a second track to elongate the cue. You can do almost anything with underscore music as long as you maintain a consistent tempo. Listening to an out-of-tempo piece of music will disturb you subconsciously even though you may not be aware of a melodic change. The music editor must listen to the harmonics as well as the melody line when a cut has to be made. An intercut will be impossible if, even though the melody continues unbroken, the harmonic, underlying elements such as strings or brass are disrupted. Tracking is challenging. With the correct music, if it weren't so frustrating, it might even be considered fun.

PITFALLS OF TRACKING

Tracking music for a feature film or television production has subtle implications, far beyond the obvious challenge of the editing of music. In many instances, the director and the film editor will have selected music to temporarily underscore a scene or sequence while still editing the film. In other instances, the temporary music will be added after the completion of the editing. This generally takes place after the music spotting session with the composer. To combine any music with the dialogue track, a temp dub is necessary. During this temp dub, the producer will be extremely opinionated and vocal concerning the music. Is the temp music contributing to the emotions of the scene? Should there be more or less music? Is it the right type of orchestration? Producers will see areas to be underscored other than the scenes designated at the spotting session, and the composer will have to be notified. The temporary dub will be completed only when the producer is completely satisfied that the music is working properly.

The producer now has a personal vested interest in the music, as he has been able virtually to perfect each cue to his liking. When the mandatory exhibitions start, the producer and director, with each additional running, will hear this temporary track music over and over and over again. If these runnings are successful, some of the credit is attributed to the music. This is called falling in love with the temp track. Everyone gets comfortable with the temporary music—but the composer has yet to score the project. It doesn't matter what the composer writes; the producer and the director, when they hear the new original music in the picture, will have to make an emotional adjustment, regardless of how well the new music accommodates the scene.

In many instances, the use of the temporary track will inadvertently create a very uncomfortable situation for a composer. An effort on the part of the music editor to underplay a scene with a small group, so as to allow the composer to top this easily using a full orchestra, will fall flat if the producer falls in love with the sparse music. If the composer scores the scene with a full orchestra, the producer might even insist that the music be reorchestrated.

Thus, composers enjoy temporary music tracks about as much as one enjoys waiting for the dentist's pick to find a cavity. Some adamantly refuse to view a film or video if there is any temporary music in the project, as it might influence their musical interpretation. In one such spotting session, some tracked music was inadvertently left in the picture; when this scene started to play, the composer left the projection room and said he would return when the music scene played out. At the opposite extreme, some composers will request a video with the temporary music included so that they can get a feel for the direction they should take in writing their original score.

· 15 ·

Sync License

GETTING THE SYNC LICENSE

An important part of a productions's music consists of songs previously written and recorded. Permission (licenses) to use this
music must be obtained. The specific form of this permission
depends on how the music will be used. For example, when the
script calls for a performance of (not a recording of) a popular song
from the year 1940, the producer will assign the music supervisor or
associate producer the task of acquiring a list of songs for that year.
This is not a difficult chore, as there are music reference books
listing every song that became popular in any given time period.
The producer or director will select a song or songs from that list,
and then the associate producer or music supervisor will contact a
music clearance agency or the publishers to get a quote on the cost
of a *sync license* for each of those songs.

A music sync license indicates that the producer has purchased
from the publisher the rights to use the publisher's song in a
production. This payment for the sync license will include the
publisher's, composer's, and lyricist's compensation. Every song
not in the public domain has a publisher, and that publisher has
the right to allow or disallow the performance of the song in the

visual medium. A production company may negotiate with the publisher directly or, safer yet, contact a music clearance house to handle the financial negotiations. When this fee is paid, the publisher will authorize a sync license for that song or songs to be issued to the production company.

One type of agreement with the publisher does not permit the use of a commercial recording of the song. Rather, the song must be rerecorded with the scoring orchestra or used in a different fashion. The song could be sung a cappella by an actor, or the lyrics could be a spoken part of the dialogue.

The cost quotation from a publisher for this type of license gives the production company permission for the song to be played, sung, or quoted, either in an on-camera performance or as rerecorded source or underscore. It does not include the use of a commercial recording.

The dominating factor influencing a publisher's decision to allow one of its tunes to be heard in a production is how the tune will be used in the picture. Will it be sung or played under a scene that is objectionable to the publisher or composer because of violence, sex, or perhaps story content? If you were the composer of "Cry Me a River," for example, you wouldn't want your song to play over a brutal beating of a small child or any pictorially unsavory scene.

In granting permission and setting fees, a publisher will also consider how important a specific song is to a production. For example, if a song will be used as source music, perhaps emanating from a jukebox as background for a conversation in an ice cream parlor, then the publisher knows that it has to be reasonable, as the song is only emphasizing an era, and other songs from other publishers could be substituted. If the song is used for the main title and played thematically throughout the picture, then it is recognized as an integral part of the project and the sync fee will be much higher.

Another factor is the number of times and the duration of time that the music will be heard in the production.

COMMERCIAL RECORDINGS

The acquisition of a sync license to use a commercial recording by a popular singer or orchestral group in a production is more complicated and necessitates payments to the recording company, musicians, and vocal artist or artists as well as the composer and the publisher. When a composer's or lyricist's estate is involved, obtaining this sync license can become complex because heirs have to be located and their releases obtained.

This complexity has resulted in the formation of music clearance companies. It becomes their responsibility to track down a publisher who might have gone out of business or sold out to another publisher. They also ensure the proper payment of fees to all individuals or companies involved in the ownership of a song.

Sync fees for commercial recordings can be upsettingly high. Using a well-known song to set just the right mood for your picture can easily cost in the five-figure range. All composition and publishing fees should be negotiated prior to any use of the song in a production. There are many horror stories of writers integrating a song title into a script (not even a song that is sung or performed), or of an actor casually ad libbing or humming a well-known song, to make even the most cavalier production company sit up and take notice. In these cases, the publishers will go after the production company with fervor. Such lack of awareness or casual neglect on the part of a production company may cost tens of thousands of dollars if any of the publisher's song is used and integrated into the production without proper notification and payment of sync fees. The production company will face an injunction and will either have to pay any fee demanded by the publisher, reshoot the scene with a different piece of music, or cancel the release.

Some songs are simply unavailable to the motion picture or video industry for various business or legal reasons. An example might be an estate's denying the use of any of a recording artist's songs because of a contractual agreement with a certain production company for the artist's life story. Or a song about a city might be held in reserve because of plans to use it as thematic material for another picture. A pending legal battle over mechanical or compositional rights can prohibit the use of a song. These and other, more subtle reasons create the need for music clearing houses.

MECHANICALS

If an existing recording of a song is requested, then there are more complications. In addition to the sync fee for the publisher and the songwriter/composer, there is a fee for the *mechanicals*: the recording company, the vocal artist, and the musicians who played on the original recording.

Let us imagine that in a preproduction meeting it was decided that a recording of Phineas Foghorn singing "Red Right Returning" over the main title will set the tone and give the production the exact feeling it requires. The associate producer contacts a music clearance company, which runs a cost factor. The publishing company will issue a sync license for one use of the complete song for $3,500. (This includes the compositional fee.) The recording company, which produced and paid for the original recording session and has a contractual agreement with the performing artist who sang the lyrics, will grant permission to use its recording for $20,000, (This fee covers the recording company and the artist.) There were 42 musicians used on the original recording session, and they will have to be repaid at the current rate for a three-hour record session; that comes to roughly $6,500. For a total of around $30,000, the original recording can be slipped into this project. Although this example is fictitious and a bit far-fetched, it still represents the basic fact that inescapable costs are likely to be incurred.

When an original commercial recording is wanted and the mechanical fees are too expensive, an alternative is to have a composer or arranger write a similar arrangement and record the song using a vocalist who does sound-alike renditions. There are vocal specialists who can duplicate the vocal sound and style characteristics of almost any singer. This recording of the song could be included as part of the scheduled postproduction underscore session, nullifying the need for an additional musician call. The sync fees will have to be paid but the cost of the mechanicals will be eliminated.

This has been a common practice in the past. In today's circumstances, however, production companies have legitimate concerns about the legality of this practice. Before recording sound-alike voices, they want to ensure that there will be no legal complications upon release of the film or video.

Occasionally, a recording company will give free access or even pay a production company to insert its current recording group in a production for the group's promotional purposes. One never knows when hearing a popular tune in a film or videotape production, what the producer had to pay for the sync and mechanical fees. Some major studios have their own recording labels, which gives them outright access to any number of popular songs and recordings. There are so many contingencies in the procurement of popular records in a picture that each case has its own unique story. For the protection of the production company, these negotiations should take place well in advance of the recordings' use in a production.

The fee also differs depending on the market of exhibition. A sync license for a domestic television exhibition is less than one for worldwide rights. For a theatrical sync license that will include video cassettes plus cable channel plus satellite transmission, with rights in perpetuity, the price from the publisher increases, with each additional right raising the cost requested.

One caveat: Don't even consider a song, tune, or recording without a thorough investigation of all of the cost factors.

PUBLIC DOMAIN

Not all tunes have to be cleared with a sync license. The term *public domain* indicates that the work or works of an artist have passed from private ownership by their estate into the world culture. These works can now be performed or reproduced without having to pay either a compositional or a publishing fee. Public domain thus includes an entire era of early American songs and the majority of the great classical compositions, whose copyrights have expired. In the 1940s, when ASCAP was the sole representative organization for songwriters, there was a holdout on any of its songs being performed on the radio, so the only tunes one would hear were all in public domain. (BMI was formed at this time to break the impasse.)

In the United States, a law was passed in 1978 specifying that a work would revert to the classification of public domain upon the fiftieth year afer the composer's death. Prior to this, a 28-year copyright period started with the publication of the material. Then, either publishers or songwriters would renew the copyright or a member of the songwriter's estate would renew it, to prohibit the work from moving into the public domain.

A work might be public domain in the United States and still be under copyright laws in European countries. Foreign countries have varying periods before copyright on a work expires. It cannot be taken for granted that the copyright has expired simply because the author or composer has been dead for a given number of years, as an heir to the composer's estate could have renewed the copyrights. The legal ramifications should be carefully studied, and this is another reason for the existence of music clearance houses.

As an example of public domain, if you were to use an old recording of the Stephen Foster tune "I Dream of Jeannie with the Light Brown Hair," because the tune is in the public domain, you would have no pulisher's cost. However, the mechanicals still have to be paid—that is, the recording company and the musicians. Some of the musicians may be dead and the payment will then go into the family trust. If the musicians are impossible to locate, a payment is made to a fund at the musicians' union. You can imagine the complications that arise when one tries to locate recording companies that have transferred ownership and been out of business for many years. The difficulty of locating composers or contacting their estates to establish true ownership of the material and then obtaining a release from them as legal owners furthers the value of using a music clearance house for this research.

The situation can be even more complex. The song "Happy Birthday," for example, has a melody that is in public domain, but its lyrics are still under copyright. That's why low-budget productions, when shooting a birthday party scene, feature the singing of "For He's a Jolly Good Fellow" instead. The melody and the lyrics of that song are both in public domain, and therefore there is no cost factor for a sync license. Remember—before using it, check it out!

MUSIC LIBRARIES

Library music (so-called *canned music*) is used when the budget for a project is too low to cover either a composer or a music scoring session. For a fee, music libraries allow the use of their music while retaining the compositional and publishing rights. In essence, this means that the music used for your project will be the same as the music used by many others on similar productions. The music editor will proceed in the same fashion as is required for a temporary dub, with the difference being that this selected music will remain permanently in the program.

Some music libraries are very diversified in their selections, whereas others are more specific in their musical material. Either way, there are some restrictions on the use of library music. The musicians' union has negotiated an agreement with the producers' association regarding the use of canned music in television and motion pictures. If any part of a project produced under a collective bargaining agreement has been scored by union musicians, no canned music can be integrated into the score. The only exception to this rule exists with mechanically made music: organ grinder, calliope, music box, and the like.

Some library music has been recorded abroad by foreign musicians who are not subject to any of the labor or producers' agreements. This music has been specifically written to be applicable for tracking. The recordings contain material for main titles, end titles, play-ons, humorous bridges, sad bridges, play-offs, love scenes, chase scenes, fight scenes, tension, shock chords, passage of time, epic grandeur, Western atmosphere, and variations on these, all thematically based and orchestrated to give continuity to the musical sound.

Music libraries also have specialty music: ethnic, calliope, organ grinder, marching bands, modern day and period bands, and special musical sounds. These include tree bells, cymbal crashes, drum rolls, harp glissandos, cocktail piano, tack piano, period tunes in public domain, and just about any imaginable musical request.

The music and the publishing rights are owned outright by the music library. The music library will set a price for the use of the music either by the needle drop (a price for each time a selection is used) or as a blanket price, depending on the project (feature or television, documentary or industrial) and the length of the production. Prices will vary for a half-hour, one-hour, two-hour, or mini-series program.

There are worldwide rights, television rights, cable rights, satellite rights, limited-time rights, perpetuity rights, and many other kinds of rights to be considered when purchasing library music to use in a project. Commercials, documentaries, industrials, educationals, and so on have a rate category separate from that for feature films and television programs.

These libraries are constantly updating their material, and a very creditable tracking performance can be obtained with their music.

Afterword

This industry, by its nature, is an ever-changing, innovative medium, which nourishes and succors the creativity that gives the industry its lifeblood—sometimes leading the public's taste and sometimes following it. It is the ultimate propaganda medium, reflecting moral, ethical, and other trends in our society. It attracts some of the most brilliant creative minds in the world, as it is the ultimate in interpretive expression (that's a pedantic phrase for the word *fun*). If you are tremendously successful, your rewards are personal gratification, personal recognition, and very often financial independence. With such rewards at stake, it is no small wonder that this is so attractive an industry.

The modus operandi of the industry is in the throes of rapid technological changes. In film, the sacred moviolas have given way to flat-bed eight-plate editing machines. Videotape editing bays are used for most television situation comedies. Sound effects are sampled (recorded) for keyboard instruments to be played against a videotape of either a film or video program, with the sound being laid down on 24-, 32-, or 48-track tape machines for the prelay, sweetening, or film dubbing stage.

Music editors are using a variety of electronic equipment and computerized programs for preparing breakdown notes for a composer and installing streamers and clicks on videotape for a scoring session. Modems and fax machines are used to transfer information from the Cue System or Spellbinder directly to a composer over telephone lines.

Music and the instruments used to make a musical sound are in a constant state of change and expansion. Our current generation has been inundated with electronic music—plug in and play. Producers and directors, in keeping with these trends, are requesting that composers include synthesized sounds or write synthesized scores for their pictures. A period picture, a traditional Western, or an ethnic picture would seem to demand acoustic instruments, as there were no electronic instruments in the old West, or prior to the 1940s, or in remote parts of Africa. But this is a purist's viewpoint, and awards have been given to period pictures with integrated synthesized sounds, *Chariots of Fire* for one.

The industry continues to operate on the basis of a producer's or director's taste regarding the music that will be used in a production. If a producer's twelve-year-old daughter raves about a musical rock group called the Bleached Blonde Surf Bombers, the producer will insist on hiring that group to do the underscore for his production. This is a dangerous trend, as the producer can negate the art of scoring and may assume that a musician is a musician and that anyone can quickly make the adjustment from commercial recordings to underscoring a picture. Even if a group is tremendously successful in the commercial recording field, assuming that they can underscore a picture is like asking a podiatrist to perform brain surgery because "a doctor is a doctor."

Those producers and directors who do not respect the expertise of the professional composer will find their productions exploited by individual performers or music groups—not deliberately, but because the individual or group does not understand the function or subtleties of underscore music in pictures.

A decision can be made to use a traditional acoustic score, an acoustic score integrating electronic sounds, or a totally electronic score. There are all types of keyboard synthesizers adding a variety of different sounds and sound effects that give composers an enormous diversity in augmenting their scores.

Digital sound is now in the mainstream of recordings. Sounds are stored by numbers using extremely complex technology. (I have been told that the only person who completely understands this system lives in an inaccessible cave somewhere in Japan and, at this time, will no longer communicate with anyone else on this planet.) With the sound being held by numbers, it will someday be possible to record digitally and, using a telephone modem, send the recording to another modem anywhere in the world without any loss of clarity. Ma Bell's lines are not yet that static-free, but who is to say they won't be soon?

Two manufacturers, Sony and Mitsubishi, seem to be vying for the lead in cornering this digital market. There has yet to be a digital standardization in the music business. Sony's original 24-track digital recorder is now obsolescent as the new 48-track has become operational. Mitsubishi's 32-track digital recorder will undoubtedly be superseded by a 64-track.

The use of the synclavier, Kurzweil, and other keyboard instruments that reproduce, not just emulate, the sound of any acoustical or electronic instrument by a system called *sampling* has become an integral part of a film scoring session. These electronic instruments are as real a threat to an acoustic musician as automation is to the factory worker. An educated ear can tell the difference between a performance by a sampled orchestra and that of an acoustical orchestra. But it seems that only the purists are concerned.

It remains to be seen where technological advances will take us and what effects they will have on people involved with music. But regardless of future developments, there are business and technical considerations that still must be adhered to when dealing with picture or videotape underscoring: the sync pulse, SMPTE time code, playbacks, dub downs, transfers, licenses, clearances, and the like are not apt to change in the near future.

One final thought: It remains my hope that this minor exposure to the complexities of including music in a film or video production will be of some help in avoiding the obvious pitfalls. (The subtle ones will get you anyway.)

So have fun—and slip in some music.

Glossary

Accelerando (Mus.) A gradual change of meter from a slower to a faster tempo within a musical composition.

Act off A television term denoting the end of an act where the picture fades or cuts to black prior to the commercial break.

Act out Alternative term for *Act off.*

Act on Television term denoting the first scene of a program or any scene opening after a commercial break.

Adapter (Mus.) A musician who compositionally adjusts an existing theme to fit a picture cue.

ADR Automated Dialogue Replacement.

Ambience The sound or tone of a room or interior of a building.

Answer print The first print made from the cut negative.

Arrangement (Mus.) The written instrumental parts of a piece of music.

Arranger (Mus.) A musician who writes the harmonics and instrumental parts for the voicing of a musical piece.

ASCAP The American Society of Composers, Authors, and Publishers.

Baffles Sound-absorbing panels designed to help control and keep sounds isolated in recording studios.

BMI Broadcast Music Incorporated.

Breakdown notes The minute timing in seconds and tenths of seconds of a scene to be underscored. This includes prefacing the scene leading into the cue, the start of the music, describing the locale, a timing of the action, a word-for-word dialogue timing including pauses, and the end of the cue. Any statements regarding the music made by the producer or composer during the spotting session are also included.

Bridge (Mus.) A piece of transitional music connecting two scenes.

Bumper (TV) A short piece of film usually seen before and after a commercial break identifying the program being viewed.

Burn-in Names of places, dates, subtitles, and the like, not part of the negative but superimposed on the release print or burned in to a dupe negative.

Capstan A smooth metallic drive wheel in a tape-recording machine.

Cartage (Mus.) The pickup and delivery of musical instruments to and from a recording session.

Channel A subdivision on a reel of magnetic tape representing one recording stripe or channel.

Classical metronome A mechanical box with 39 available tempos from 40 beats to 208 beats per minute. Used by musicians to maintain tempo.

Colors Composers refer to musical orchestrations as being a *warm color* (trombones, cellos, or midrange woodwinds played with feeling), or a *cold color* (high violin section, tense with no vibrato).

Composite track Any track that incorporates more than one element.

Conductor (Mus.) The leader of the orchestra, who usually stands on a podium and establishes tempo by making definitive motions with a baton.

Contractor (Mus.) Orchestra manager.

Copyist (Mus.) A person who copies instrumental parts from the composer's score, transcribing them for the individual players.

Cracks (Mus.) Any played or sung note that is out of pitch. This expression comes from the cracks (separation between the keys) on a piano.

Cue (Mus.) A designation given to a scene or area of picture to be covered musically.

Dailies West Coast term for the previous day's shooting. (On the East Coast they are called *rushes*.)

Dialogue track A sound track of the production recorded sound.

Digital metronome An electronic box with metronomic settings based on frames of film and a frame's division into eighths.

Domestic Any English-speaking country.

Double (Mus.) An orchestra member who plays more than one instrument.

Down beat (Mus.) The first beat of any bar of music.

Dry (Mus.) No reverberation included.

Dubbing The mixing or blending together of tracks.

Dubbing units Reels containing dialogue, sound effects, and music tracks, programmed to cover specific areas in the picture.

Dupe A shortened term for *duplication*. Used when referring to any picture that duplicates the work print.

Earwig A small radio receiver that fits into the ear.

Emulsion The surface of the film with the emulsion ingredient that holds the photographed image.

Episodic Usually refers to one program of a television series that has a consistent daily, weekly, or monthly, time schedule.

EPS Electronic Post Synchronization (East Coast term for Automated Dialogue Replacement).

Final cut In editing, this is the polished, completed work print.

Final dub The dub that completes the sound track that will be heard on the theater release prints.

Foley Recorded footsteps and movement.

Foreign Any non-English-speaking country.

Footage counter A device with numbers that indicate the footage from the start mark of a reel of film.

Framing The proper positioning of film or videotape in the projection aperture.

Free clicks (Mus.) Clicks heard by the musicians that set a tempo and are not included as part of the score.

Free timing (Mus.) Music recorded to clock or film without benefit of clicks.

Full-coat   A 35 mm film that is covered with a magnetic coating used for the recording of sound.

Inflections   (Mus.) Increases or decreases in volume to effect musical nuances.

Intercut   Cutting together of two different scenes or musical phrases.

Librarian   (Mus.) Keeper and distributor of the written orchestral parts.

Lip sync   The ability to duplicate the exact lip movement necessary to mime or mimic a prerecorded song or line of dialogue.

Live shoot   On the production shooting set recording, the music as the musicians perform on camera.

Loop   An old-fashioned term for ADR or EPS.

Main title   That area of a production that shows the title of the production and lists some preeminent credits.

Master track   A track that contains any original recording.

Meter   (Mus.) Number of beats in a bar.

Metric consistency   (Mus.) Same number of beats per bar for entire piece.

Mixer   A sound person who records or blends sounds together.

Mixing panel   A console containing electronic sound controls for use on scoring stages and dubbing rooms.

Monaural   Single-track recording.

MOS   Minus Optical Sound (colloquially, Mid-Out Sound). Any scene shot silent.

Moviola   A synchronous machine used to edit film, dialogue, sound effects and music, while viewing the picture and listening to the sound.

Music Contractor   The individual who calls the musicians for a scoring session and is considered the orchestra manager.

Music editor   The person who writes the spotting notes and breakdown notes, and prepares the film or video with streamers and clicks for the scoring stage. The editor also builds the recorded music into units for the dubbing or sweetening stage. When on the dubbing stage, any musical changes requested by the producer will be made by the music editor.

Music engineer   The individual responsible for the balance, tonality, and recording of the individual instruments and instrumental sections of the entire orchestra.

Music librarian   On the scoring stage, the music librarian distributes the orchestral parts to the musicians' stands and remains on the session to help with any changes and collect the music when the session is completed.

Music supervisor   A knowledgeable musician who organizes and supervises special musical material needed for the production.

Music units   Reels containing music and used on the dubbing stage.

Nagra   A quarter-inch tape recorder, with a synchronous pulse, that is used to record the production sound and can be used to run the playback.

Nuances   (Mus.) Subtleties in music to accentuate the emotions of a scene musically.

One-to-one   A direct transfer of any recorded material to duplicate itself.

Opticals   An all-encompassing term for picture fades, dissolves, wipes, montages, main and end titles, and any special film effects.

Optical click track   (Mus.) Click perforations punched in solid-based film that, when played on an optical sound machine, will create a tempo.

Optical negative   The negative created by photographing the sound of a dubbed track.

Orchestrator   (Mus.) An arranger (Usually with orchestra.)

Pickups   Any recording or pictorial shots needed to correct the original.

Picture editor   The individual responsible for the pictorial assembly and flow of a film or videotape program.

Pitch   (Mus.) The tonal quality of a note.

Pitch pipe   (Mus.) A harmonica-like mechanism with a complete octave of notes in perfect pitch. It is used to tune musical instruments.

Playback   (Mus.) A musical piece properly recorded on tape and used on the set for actors to simulate actual playing or singing.

Playback operator   A sound person who operates the playback machine on the shooting set.

Postproduction   The time period between the completion of photography to the final release print being accepted.

Prelay   (Video) Designating the predubbing of sound tracks in preparation for the sweetening stage.

Preproduction   The preparation time prior to the actual shooting of the film.

Prerecording   A recording made prior to the shooting of a musical scene.

Prescore   A musical scoring session to record music for a stage playback.

Print   Designates film to be printed from negative or recorded material to be transferred from sound.

Production sound mixer   The recordist on the shooting set.

Pulsation   The alternating 60-cycle current being recorded on one channel of a magnetic tape.

Punch   Hole in film or flash effect on videotape.

Quartz crystal   A crystal used in cameras and recorders.

Reproductions   (Mus.) The photocopying of the musical scores.

Rerecording stage   Another name for a *dubbing stage, sweetening stage,* or *mixing stage.*

Recordist   The person who physically handles the recording equipment to ensure that the musical instruments are being recorded on their assigned tracks at the proper level.

Release print   Applicable to film only. This is a finished composite print that is distributed to theaters for public viewing.

Residual   Monies paid from foreign and domestic performances.

Room ambience   The inherent sound quality of any room.

Rube Goldberg device   Any ridiculously overcomplex machine designed to perform a simple, basic task.

Sampling   The recording of a sound effect, or a note from a musical instrument, for the express purpose of varying the length or pitch of the sound.

Scribe   (Mus.) An instrument used to scrape the emulsion from film to create a line (streamer).

Script supervisor   The individual who keeps an accurate account of every scene photographed in the shooting of a production.

Score   (Mus.) [The] *score* (noun): Music used in a production. [To] *score* (verb): To record music for a picture production.

Scoring stage (Mus.) A room specially designed and equipped for orchestral recordings.

Seconds counter A small counter added to a moviola and sync machine that registers footage in seconds and tenths of seconds.

Single-stripe A reel of 35 mm clear-base film with a narrow stripe of magnetic tape covering a third of the picture area and running the total length of the roll. Used mainly for dialogue transfers.

Shadings See *Nuances.*

Sketch (Mus.) Music with an indicated tempo and a melody line or theme written out. Instructions for instrumentation and harmonics are indicated but not orchestrated.

SMPTE The Society of Motion Picture Technicians and Engineers.

Sound effects Any noise that contributes to the realism of the picture.

Sound effects editor An editor who works with sound effects, dialogue, and Foley.

Source (Mus.) Denotes music emanating from a source: an on-camera musical performance, a radio, a television set, a jukebox, a calliope, Muzak, or anything else that can be a source of music.

Spotting notes Notes made after the spotting session, containing the starts and stops of the cues to be underscored, along with an overall timing and brief description of the scene.

Sprocket holes Holes along both sides of 35 mm film and on one side of 16 mm film (none on videotape).

Start frame Any agreed-on frame to set a footage or seconds counter at zero.

Stem One of the magnetic recording track areas on the dubbed master track.

Stop frame The ability to hold frame on a videotape machine.

Stock footage Stock libraries maintain film footage of current and historical events, scenic locations, animals, insects, earthquakes, fires, floods, cars, accidents, stunts and special effects, and the like. These scenes are for sale by the foot.

Streamer (Mus.) A visual line moving from one side of the screen to the other.

Stylus (Mus.) An instrument used to scrape a narrow line in a piece of film in order to make a streamer.

Sweetening stage Video term for *rerecording stage, dubbing stage,* or *mixing stage.*

Swimming (Mus.) Instrumental sounds moving within the orchestra and distorting clear resolution.

Sync license Every song, except those in public domain, is owned by a publisher. For a given fee, a sync license, permitting a specified use of the publisher's song in a film or video production, will be issued by the publisher.

Synchronization Refers to sound running at the same speed and being in sync with the picture.

Sync pulse Any electronic pulsation that is recorded on tape and used to control speed.

Take Refers to photographed or recorded material that is to be printed.

Tape In every instance this term refers to magnetic recording tape.

Tempo Number of beats per minute.

Thematic (Mus.) A musical tune or phrase that is used over and over in variations of speed and colorations to give a thematic cohesiveness to a production.

Three-stripe A reel of 35 mm clear-base film with three narrow stripes of magnetic recording tape.

Time code A visually displayed (or hidden) group of numbers indicating time and frame number on videotape.

Timings (Mus.) Descriptions of actions and dialogue noted by seconds and tenths of seconds on the music breakdown sheets.

Tracks General term for any recorded sound material.

Tracking (Mus.) To select, tailor, and place a piece or pieces of music in a picture.

Underscore (Mus.) Music designed for the emotional enhancement of a production.

Video master The videotape containing all the original recorded material.

Wild (Mus.) Recording a musical cue without the benefit of a projected picture.

Wow A musical passage that varies in pitch because of a transfer machine's failure to maintain speed.

Wrap The completion of any major job.

Index

Academy of Motion Picture Arts and
Sciences, 31
Accelerando, 80, 99
Address track, 28
ADR, *see* Automated dialogue
replacement
Analog recording, versus digital, 21–
22
Apologetic music, 130
Album dub down, 108–109
American Society of Composers,
Authors and Publishers
(ASCAP), 62, 135, 136, 137, 151
revenue and distribution formulas
of, 138
and two publishing companies,
139
Annie, 41
Apocalypse Now, 126
Associate producer, 9–10
Augmenting, 97; *see also*
Sweetening
Auricle, 79, 80, 100
Automated dialogue replacement
(ADR), 12, 116, 119, 123, 124, 134

Baffles, 83–84
Bar, 37, 39
Bar chart/graph, 38
Beat(s), 37
free, 75
Best Song Score, 31
Boom person, 40
Brass, 38
Breakdown notes, 60, 69–74
Broadcast Music Incorporated
(BMI), 62, 135, 136, 137, 151
revenue and distribution formulas
of, 138
and two publishing companies, 139
The Buddy Holly Story, 51
Building
of temporary tracks, 144
of units, 112–114

Cable puller, 40
Camera move in, 129
Canned music, 152–153
Cards, 128
Cell side, of film, 25
Channels, 25

167